School Administration Series

Edited by

George D. Strayer and N. L. Engelhardt

The Strayer-Engelhardt
School Administration Series

WEALTH, CHILDREN
and
EDUCATION

by

John K. Norton
Professor of Education
Teachers College, Columbia University

and

Margaret Alltucker Norton
Formerly Associate Director, Research Division
National Education Association

Bureau of Publications
Teachers College, Columbia University
New York 1937

Printed in the United States of America

MANUFACTURED BY THE HADDON CRAFTSMEN, INC.

CAMDEN, N. J.

EDITORS' INTRODUCTION

LARGER participation by the Federal Government in the financing of public education has been advocated by many students of the problem of educational finance during the past two decades. This advocacy is based upon the known facts of the lack of significant educational opportunity for hundreds of thousands of American boys and girls and upon the increasing evidence of the disparity among the states in ability to support schools.

The obligation of the nation to provide support for public education is fundamental. Schools and other means of education have been recognized from the beginning of our history as necessary for the maintenance of the nation and for the prosperity of its people. The founding fathers stated in no uncertain terms their belief that democratic government was dependent upon the enlightenment of all of the people. As Madison put it,

A popular government without popular information or the means of acquiring it is but a prologue to a farce or a tragedy, or perhaps both. Knowledge will forever govern ignorance; and a people who mean to be their own governors must arm themselves with the power which knowledge gives.

It was in line with this early appreciation of the importance of education that action was taken by the Congress of the United States in the support of schools. As the nation expanded beyond the thirteen original colonies, land was set aside in each state by the Federal Government for the support of common schools. Later moneys and land were provided for the support of higher education. In more recent years money has been granted for the development of agricultural experiment stations, for vocational education, for the rehabilitation of those injured in the Great War, for persons disabled in industry, for a program of education of youth and adults through the extension service of the Department of Agriculture, and for many other purposes.

In the program of recovery money has been granted for the construction of school buildings, for the employment of teachers in schools which would otherwise have been closed, for the partial support of students in high schools, colleges, and universities, for the instruction of adults, and for the establishment of nursery schools.

But all of the measures taken up to the present time are insufficient to meet the legitimate demand for an acceptable program of education for all children and youths throughout the nation. The lack of educational opportunity may be expressed in several ways. There are children in the United States for whom no school at all or a very minimum term of three or four months is provided. There are others who are taught by teachers with inadequate preparation. There are still others for whom the necessary books and other educational supplies are wanting. There are hundreds of thousands enrolled in schools in which the opportunities provided are limited to a traditional school curriculum which takes little or no account of the special aptitudes or abilities of those who vary in intelligence, in interests, or in vocational outlook from the selected group for whom the schools were originally organized.

These facts which have been amply demonstrated must give pause to anyone who seeks through education to provide for an intelligent electorate or who believes that through the exercise of the franchise we may preserve our democracy.

Children who are denied education in the poorer sections of the country today will live in other parts of the United States and will be responsible for government, local, state, and national, in the years which lie ahead. There is no large city in the United States in which the birth rate is sufficient to maintain even a stationary population. From those areas in which educational opportunity is most meager there will be recruited the population of our cities.

The authors of this treatise have been engaged for the past few years in a continuing study of the ability of the states to support education. They have, as well, participated in many inquiries concerning the lack of educational opportunity both before 1929 and since that time. They have in this volume brought together the results of their own researches and those of many other investigators dealing with the problems of educational finance. In the discussion and more particularly in the evidence presented in the tables contained in this volume on *Wealth, Children, and Education* will be found the answer to the question, "What must we do to provide education for all of the children of all of the people?"

There was a time when it was possible for one who was opposed to further federal support for education to propose that such support was not needed because the lack of ability to support an adequate program of education in each of the states had not been demonstrated. From the analyses which appear herein, based upon unimpeachable evidence, one who seeks the truth will be forced to the conclusion that we may not continue to depend wholly upon local and state support for education.

The present inadequacy or denial of educational opportunity to American boys and girls will most certainly continue unless in the light of the facts available we develop a national program in line with our current economic situation. The United States is one great economic unit. Business and industry are organized on a national basis. Our economic interdependence, the mobility of our population, the lack of resources in one geographic area and the wealth available in another—all point to the necessity for support on a national basis.

It is high time that the facts concerning the situation be made known throughout the length and breadth of the land. Pertinent data are presented in this volume in detail and yet in such simple form that anyone who doubts the necessity for national action can find the evidence upon which to base sound judgment. The discussion and the accompanying evidence are presented as a challenge to all who believe that through education we have the only certain means for the preservation of our liberties and the continuance of our democratic form of government. The only time the children of this generation may enjoy educational opportunity is now. A denial of educational opportunity at any time in a democracy cannot but result in disaster in the years which lie ahead.

GEORGE D. STRAYER

N. L. ENGELHARDT

January 29, 1937

ACKNOWLEDGMENTS

THIS publication is the culmination of a series of research projects on which the authors have worked for a period of years. The researches of other investigators have also been drawn upon. Acknowledgment of this indebtedness is made through frequent footnotes.

The authors are greatly indebted to the Committee on Government and Educational Finance of the American Council on Education for funds for clerical assistance and for the publication of certain preliminary investigations upon which this study draws. The funds at the disposal of the Committee for this purpose were supplied by the Carnegie Corporation of New York. This indispensable financial assistance is gratefully acknowledged. The interest and constructive criticisms of members of the Committee as the study progressed were both encouraging and helpful. The cordial assistance and advice of George F. Zook, President, American Council on Education, during the later phases of the study have been most valuable.

The assistance and encouragement of the late Henry Suzzallo played a crucial role in the early phases of the investigation. His outstanding leadership in developing the Report of the National Advisory Committee on Education and in clarifying national thought concerning the relation of the Federal Government to the administration and financing of education in the United States is recognized by all students of this phase of political science.

Grateful acknowledgment is also made to the Works Progress Administration for assistance in connection with some of the extensive preliminary statistical tabulations and calculations upon which certain phases of this investigation depend. This work was registered as Project No. 65-97-295, Sub-project 4 of the U. S. Works Progress Administration of New York City.

The effective help of Miss Evelyn M. Horton, statistician, Institute of Educational Research, Teachers College, Columbia University, in the final checking of statistical calculations is acknowledged with appreciation.

Recognition is made of the great influence which the Educational Finance Inquiry, directed by George D. Strayer, has had upon research in the field of educational finance during the last decade. This publication and many of the researches upon which it draws owe their original impetus to the Educational Finance Inquiry.

While grateful acknowledgment of assistance by individuals and by organizations is made, the authors accept full responsibility for the data and conclusions of this study.

JOHN NORTON
MARGARET A. NORTON

CONTENTS

LIST OF TABLES

LIST OF FIGURES

INTRODUCTION

GEORGE WASHINGTON in his Farewell Address urged his countrymen . to look upon the promotion of institutions for the general diffusion of knowledge as an object of primary concern. It has long been a principle of American life that adequate educational facilities are essential to the effective operation of democratic government. The validity of this principle has been emphasized as the growing complexity of a dynamic civilization and the interdependence of its factors have brought government into ever-widening areas of our life. If "the instruction of the American people in every kind of knowledge" was essential to the effective operation of democratic government in the eighteenth century, how much more essential it is in the twentieth!

It is a well-established fact, however, that there are today many school districts in the country which are not maintaining adequate educational facilities even according to very meager standards. Nor can this situation be charged to that popular cause of all evil, the depression. The depression doubtless added to the educational slums of the nation, but it did not bring them into existence.

Why are there areas in which American children and youths are being denied satisfactory educational opportunity? A variety of circumstances are involved. Undoubtedly, however, one of the most potent and immediate factors in the situation is finance. The funds available for the support of educational facilities in our educational slums are more limited than experience has shown is essential to the maintenance of even an acceptable minimum of educational opportunity.

This fact, which is adequately documented in later sections of this study, raises a series of general and specific questions. Is our national economy as a whole unable to finance the education of all the nation's children? Are there particular states or sections which are unable to pay for a suitable educational program? How far is the denial of educational opportunity in certain areas associated with lack of willingness, rather than with financial inability to pay for schools? Can educational underprivilege be removed in the United States if all states and sections of the nation put their financial houses in order by adopting modern tax systems and by allocating a suitable proportion of resulting revenue to the financing of education? What social consequences may be expected to follow the indefinite continuance of extreme differences in educational opportunity offered children in different states and sections of the nation?

These questions have long been the subject of debate. The factual information upon which satisfactory answers might be based has been lacking. In recent years, however, a series of careful studies has been completed which permit the use of facts, as opposed to opinion and prejudice, in the study of these issues.

The purpose of this document is to set forth in simple and succinct form present evidence on the questions listed above. It should be stated at the outset that this evidence is neither complete nor final. The economic and other elements in the situation are so unwieldy and complex that their measurement in a wholly satisfactory manner is extremely difficult. Nevertheless, sufficient progress has been made in the technique of measuring the concepts involved to permit a cautious presentation of figures and at least a tentative statement of conclusions. These conclusions are believed to have large significance for the development of social policy in the United States, particularly as it is tied up with the maintenance of an acceptable level of educational opportunity in all parts of the nation.

Wealth, Children, and Education

CHAPTER I

THE ECONOMIC ABILITY OF THE UNITED STATES TO FINANCE EDUCATION

THE standard of education which may be maintained by a nation, like other elements of its standard of living, is inescapably related to the economic productivity of that nation and its choices with reference to use of its income. Ability to consume goods and services, whether purchased privately or publicly, implies productive capacity. Expenditure for any purpose involves allocation of a portion of the nation's income for the support of the enterprise involved.

Discussion of national provision of adequate financial support for the educational institutions of the country, therefore, necessitates consideration of two questions. First, What is the capacity of the nation to produce? Second, What is the probability that the various factors involved will result in an adequate allocation of the products of economic productivity to the support of education? Each of these questions will be considered in turn.

The best measurement of the actual productive capacity of the United States is the increasingly meaningful estimates of national income made by various reliable statistical agencies. The term "income" is a highly complex concept.[1] The methods used in estimating the various elements which when totaled constitute the annual income of the nation differ considerably. Also, the items included in the estimates of income vary. This accounts for the fact that the estimates of total national income made by various statistical agencies frequently differ considerably.

For present purposes, however, it may be said that there are two general definitions of income—income produced and income paid out. The national income produced is the aggregate value of all commodities produced and services rendered less the value of materials and capital used in the process of production. Income paid out may be defined as the amounts paid to individuals for all productive ser-

[1] See: U. S. Department of Commerce, Bureau of Foreign and Domestic Commerce, *National Income in the United States, 1929–35*, pp. 1–2. Government Printing Office, Washington, D. C., 1936.

vices. Income produced and income paid out do not total the same aggregate in any one year. If payments by all business enterprises are less than the aggregate net production, then a portion of the net product may go into surplus accounts, representing business savings. If by drafts on these resources the income paid out is more than the income produced, the difference may be termed business losses. The amount of income paid out may be arrived at by adding business savings, or deducting business losses, from the estimates of income produced.

Estimates of national income and of national productive capacity, for the years 1929 to 1934 inclusive, together with the amounts expended for tax-supported schools and colleges in the same years, are presented statistically in Table 1 and in graphic form in Figure I. The estimates of national income were made by the United States Department of Commerce. The estimates of productive capacity are taken from the comprehensive investigation of the Brookings Institution[2] of Washington, D. C., which sought to arrive at a scientific estimate of America's capacity to produce. The basis of the latter estimates is briefly stated as follows:

. . . we are concerned not with the theoretical maxima of production but with practical results which could be obtained under conditions of operation with which we have had actual experience. We are not attempting to calculate productive performances that might be brought about under ideal conditions but simply to measure how much more product we could turn out if the demand of the market were such as to keep our plant and labor employed as fully as they could be under accepted hours of labor and with proper standards of plant maintenance. . . . In our analysis we have endeavored to arrive at capacity estimates that are obtainable under the *practical operating conditions* which exist. . . . The analysis by which we have proceeded to these final conclusions has been sufficiently buttressed by statistical measurement at all major points, and our final estimates have been checked against the practical experience and criticism of technicians and business men to an extent that eliminates possibilities of serious error.[3]

On the basis of estimates thus obtained the conclusion was reached that the industrial plant of the nation was technically capable, under the conditions prevailing in 1929, of adding nineteen per cent to the actual production of that year. We were not living beyond our means in 1929. We were not trenching on our resources of capital goods or of

[2] See: Harold G. Moulton, *Income and Economic Progress*, pp. 21–23, 176. The Brookings Institution, Washington, D. C., 1935.

[3] Edwin G. Nourse and Associates, *America's Capacity to Produce*, pp. 23, 27, and 28. The Brookings Institution, Washington, D. C., 1934.

TABLE 1. POTENTIAL PRODUCTIVE CAPACITY, NATIONAL INCOME
PRODUCED AND PAID OUT, AND EXPENDITURES
FOR PUBLIC EDUCATION

(In millions of current dollars)

Item	1929	1930	1931	1932	1933	1934
Potential productive capacity [1]	$97,508	$97,508	$97,508	$97,508	$97,508	$97,508
Income produced [2]	81,034	67,917	53,584	39,545	41,889	48,561
Business savings or losses ...	2,402	− 5,015	− 8,120	− 8,817	− 3,051	− 1,628
Income paid out	78,632	72,932	61,704	48,362	44,940	50,189
Expenditures for tax-supported schools and colleges [3]	2,527	2,606	2,531	2,457	2,249	1,940
Percentage relationships:						
Potential productive capacity and educational expenditures	.0259	.0267	.0260	.0252	.0231	.0199
Income produced and educational expenditures	.0312	.0384	.0472	.0621	.0537	.0399
Income paid out and educational expenditures	.0321	.0357	.0410	.0508	.0500	.0387

[1] This is estimate of Brookings Institution for 1929, in its study of *Income and Economic Progress*. This study assumed that productive capacity remained stationary during 1929–1934.
[2] See: Robert R. Nathan, *The National Income Produced, 1929–34*, p. 2. United States Department of Commerce, Washington, D. C., November, 1935.
[3] From *Biennial Survey of Education in the United States*, United States Office of Education, Washington, D. C. Data for 1929, 1931, and 1933 are interpolations.

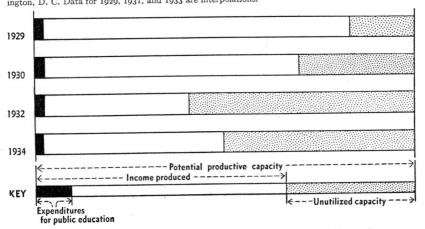

FIGURE I. Potential Productive Capacity, Income Produced, and Expenditures
for Public Education, 1929–1934
The data of this figure are from Table 1

labor. Rather, "our economic society lacked almost twenty per cent
of living up to its means."[4]

The estimates of the Brookings Institution are the most conservative which have been made. All investigations of the productive ca-

[4] *Ibid.*, p. 425.

pacity of the United States agree that production can be expanded beyond the level of the peak year, 1929. The amount to which it might be expanded, however, is placed by other investigations at a higher figure than the Brookings Institution estimates. For example, the Hoover Committee on the Elimination of Waste in Industry estimated in 1921 a waste of productive capacity in six major industries ranging from 29 per cent to almost 64 per cent.[5]

The 1933 Columbia University Commission appointed by Nicholas Murray Butler estimated, on the basis of data gathered from prominent engineers and business leaders, that production could be increased by 78 per cent if equipment and management could be improved to conform with the best current practice, and that even with existing management and equipment a 36 per cent increase would be possible.[6]

Another national survey of potential capacity, made by the New York City Housing Authority, also bases its estimates on the productivity of the existing plant. It gives $135,516,000,000, some $42,000,000,000 above the actual production of 1929, as "a minimum estimate of practical capacity."[7]

Studies of the type illustrated in the foregoing paragraphs furnish highly significant evidence concerning the ability of the nation to support education, particularly as this ability is conditioned by capacity to produce. These investigations reach the conclusion that there is no reason from an engineering or physical point of view why annual national income should not only equal that of 1929 but exceed it considerably. Ability to finance a standard of living, including a standard of educating at least comparable to that maintained in 1929, does not need to wait upon an increase in such vital prerequisites to production as machinery, labor supply, and raw materials. We already possess these means of production; the only thing lacking is the intelligent use of them. It seems reasonable that human intelligence will find a cure for the economic maladjustments responsible for the disparity between actual and potential productivity. Proposals looking in this direction are being advanced. Several economic studies suggest that a better balancing and expansion of consumer purchasing power and demand will permit at least a partial closing of the gap between actual and possible production.

[5] *Waste in Industry.* McGraw-Hill Book Company, New York, 1921.
[6] Columbia University Commission, *Economic Reconstruction.* Columbia University Press, New York, 1934.   [7] Harold Loeb, Director, *Report of the National Survey of Potential Capacity*, p. 238. New York City Housing Authority, New York City, 1935.

TABLE 2. ACTUAL PRODUCTION, POTENTIAL PRODUCTIVE CAPACITY, AND DISPARITY BETWEEN THE TWO, 1925-1934*

(In millions of 1929 dollars)

Year	Total Income Produced	Potential Productive Capacity	Disparity Between Income Produced and Potential Productive Capacity	Percentage of Potential Capacity Realized
1925	$ 75,315	$ 89,625	$ 14,310	84
1926	77,254	91,932	14,678	84
1927	78,335	93,219	14,884	84
1928	79,759	94,913	15,154	84
1929	81,940	97,508	15,568	84
1930	74,744	97,508	22,764	77
1931	66,800	97,508	30,708	69
1932	57,000	97,508	40,508	58
1933	59,000	97,508	38,508	61
1934	60,400	97,508	37,108	62
Total	$710,547	$954,737	$244,190	74

* Based on data taken from *Income and Economic Progress*, by Harold G. Moulton, p. 176. The Brookings Institution, Washington, D. C., 1935.

Enormous economic gain would have resulted from maintaining economic productivity up to the level declared to be physically possible by the conservative estimates of the Brookings Institution, as is indicated in Table 2. This table, in order to preserve comparability, has translated all sums into dollars of 1929 purchasing power. The data suggest that production totaling $244,190,000,000 was lost during the ten years 1925–1934 because of unused productive capacity. In summing up the whole situation, the Brookings Institution states:

In general, during the fourteen years, 1922–1935, the productive mechanism of the nation, by means of which our wants are supplied, may be said to have run at little more than two-thirds efficiency.[8]

Assuming that production can be brought closer to capacity, what are the conclusions concerning the financing of education? Would education receive a share of the additional income? There is no easy or simple answer to this question. A number of factors would contribute toward determining the outcome. Some of these will be briefly considered in the subsequent paragraphs.

The composition of the various economic activities, both public and private, which are reflected in estimates of national income, is determined in large measure by the choices of the people. Expenditures for all tax-supported educational institutions account for but a

[8] Harold G. Moulton, *Income and Economic Progress*, p. 30. Brookings Institution, Washington, D. C., 1935.

minor fraction of the nation's income. If the people genuinely desire to increase the educational budget, they may do so by allocating to this purpose an increasing share of the greater income which may result from a better use of our economic capacity, or even by directing a larger portion of current available economic effort toward school support.

The economic process of diverting the flow of economic energy from one or several areas of activity into channels connected with the maintenance of educational facilities is a complex one and cannot be accomplished quickly without serious dislocations.[9] Over a period of years, however, it is entirely practical, in an economy such as that which exists in the United States, for the people, if they so desire, to increase substantially the financial support of education. Such a desire, however, will have to be expressed in the form of certain definite decisions and actions, as, for example, those illustrated below.

First, it will be necessary for the American people to recognize that education is so important that it should be properly provided for in the total national budget of public and private expenditure. Some commodities and services must be forgone in order that schools may be adequately financed.

An analysis of the budget of national expenditure reveals outlays in many commercial fields which are considerably larger than those made for all educational activities. For example, nearly six and a half billion dollars have been spent annually for the following group of luxuries: [10]

Tobacco	$2,141,220,000
Soft drinks, ice cream, candy, and chewing gum	1,850,240,000
Theaters, movies, and similar amusements	1,082,790,000
Jewelry, perfumes, and cosmetics	827,740,000
Sporting goods, toys, etc.	499,660,000
Total	$6,401,650,000

The presentation of these figures does not imply that expenditures of this sort should be proscribed. Only the most austere would wish to prevent the production and consumption of a reasonable amount of

[9] George D. Strayer and Robert Murray Haig, *The Financing of Education in the State of New York*, Chap. X, "The Economic Limitations of Educational Expenditures." The Macmillan Company, New York, 1923.

[10] *Research Bulletin of the National Education Association*, Vol. VIII, No. 4, p. 180, September, 1930.

non-essentials. The size of the bill for luxury goods, however—more than twice that spent for all types of schools and colleges, both public and private—suggests that there is need for further consideration of the scale of values held by the American people as reflected in national expenditures. In developing the future policy of the nation in regard to the budgeting of its expenditures, who would call it wise to limit the educational opportunities offered children and youths, in order that we might continue to increase amounts available for such items as candy, chewing gum, tobacco, jewelry, and theater attendance?

Another national bill of large amount is that for passenger automobiles. In 1928 approximately $12,500,000,000 was expended for the purchase, operation, and upkeep of passenger automobiles.[11] This excludes the cost of motor trucks. Here again we are dealing with an important phase of national life and expenditure. Much of the money spent for automobiles is a wise investment. Some of it verges on extravagance. But wherever we may classify automobile costs, who would say that it is more important to make full provision for passenger automobile needs than for education?

The process of making up the national budget of expenditures brings school costs, a public expenditure, into frequent competition with various types of private expenditure. Because it is a public function, education along with other public enterprises often suffers from a popular misconception. The hundreds of millions of dollars spent to advertise the virtues of goods and services offered for private sale, and the ceaseless propaganda to keep taxation down to the lowest possible minimum, cause some to look upon public expenditure as mere waste. This is far from a proper view of the matter.[12] Actually, public expenditures are inherently neither less nor more productive than private expenditures. Certainly the product of an effectively operating school system in a democratic industrial society is of first-rate importance. It not only liquidates its own cost but returns handsome dividends in technical training and general intelligence, which are the foundations of economic prosperity.

Public education also competes for support with other public enterprises. Choices must be made in respect to the proportion of public revenue to be allotted to such enterprises as roads, municipal govern-

[11] *Ibid.*, p. 180.
[12] Strayer and Haig, *op. cit.*, p. 144.

TABLE 3. FEDERAL, STATE, LOCAL, AND PUBLIC SCHOOL
EXPENDITURES, 1930–1934

(In millions of dollars)

Year	AMOUNTS					PERCENTAGES			
	Total*	Federal*	State*	Local*	Public Schools and Colleges[1]	Federal	State	Local	Public Schools and Colleges
1930 ..	$13,428	$4,141	$2,223	$7,064	$2,606	30.8	16.6	52.6	19.4
1931 ..	13,516	4,172	2,367	6,977	2,531	30.9	17.5	51.6	18.7
1932 ..	14,453	5,225	2,322	6,906	2,457	36.1	16.1	47.8	17.0
1933 ..	13,316	5,264	2,141	5,911	2,249	39.5	16.1	44.4	16.9
1934 ..	15,496	7,207	2,132	6,157	1,940	46.5	13.8	39.7	12.5

* Taken from *Cost of Government in the United States 1933–1935*, p. 7. National Industrial Conference Board, 247 Park Avenue, New York City, 1936.
[1] The expenditures for public schools and colleges in this column are included in the amounts indicated in the other columns. This column merely segregates that portion of federal, state, and local governmental expenditures made for public schools and colleges. Figures are based on data collected by the United States Office of Education.

ment, relief, military services, and public works, as well as to education. If in the course of making these choices, inadequate sums are allocated for education, it will be impossible to maintain adequate schools and colleges.

Second, the adequate financing of education in the United States waits upon the establishment of a modern system for raising and distributing money for the support of this service. In most states today the financial support for schools is still largely derived from taxes similar to those employed in the eighteenth and nineteenth centuries, when wealth was more evenly distributed and existed mainly in the form of land. As a consequence securing adequate financial support for education is extremely difficult even in normal times, and becomes impossible in many communities during periods of depression.[13]

On the other hand, a system of taxation more consistent with the type of economic development which now exists in the United States has been developed by the Federal Government. This system of taxation was undoubtedly one of the factors which made it possible to increase federal expenditures substantially after the year 1930, at a time when outlays for education, dependent upon a less appropriate tax system, sharply declined. Table 3 and Figure II present data on this point. They show the gross expenditures of all governmental levels in the United States, including payments for debt retirement

[13] See: John K. Norton, "American Educational Finance," Chap. VI in *Taxation and Public Policy*, edited by Paul Studenski. Richard R. Smith, Publisher, New York, 1936.

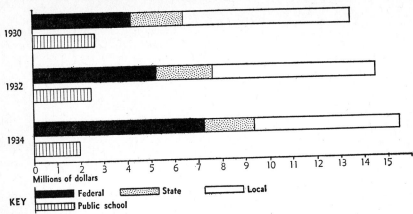

FIGURE II. Federal, State, Local, and Public School Expenditures, 1930–1934
The data of this figure are from Table 3

and federal tax refunds. In 1930 federal expenditures constituted 30.8 per cent of the total governmental bill, as compared with 46.5 per cent in 1934. During the same period, the bill for public schools and colleges decreased from 19.4 per cent to 12.5 per cent of gross governmental expenditures.

Throughout the years of the depression the Federal Government found it possible to obtain increasing sums for permanent services as well as for so-called emergency services, such as relief and public works. The 1936 budget for military purposes, for example, was the largest in peace-time history. Enterprises which happened to be financed by the Federal Government were generously supported. The federal system of taxation made it possible to realize adequate revenue, either through current taxation or through borrowing.

On the other hand, the bill for public schools and colleges in the United States was 26 per cent less in 1934 than in 1930. The trend of expenditures for public education for each year from 1924 to 1934 is shown in Table 4.

Education suffered disproportionately in the adjustments of public expenditures made during the depression. Does this reflect a reasoned decision on the part of the American people? Does it seem likely that they would have voted affirmatively, even in the depth of the depression, on the question: Shall expenditures for public education be reduced proportionately more than those for other public enterprises?

It is not a reasonable assumption that the downward trend in expenditures for educational services and the upward trend in expendi-

TABLE 4. TRENDS IN EXPENDITURES FOR PUBLIC EDUCATION IN THE UNITED STATES, 1924–1934

(Based on figures collected by the United States Office of Education)

| Year | Public Elementary and Secondary Schools | Public Universities, Colleges, and Teacher Training Institutions | Total Public Education | Index of Change 1926 = 100 | | |
				Schools (Col. 2)	Colleges (Col. 3)	Total (Col. 4)
1	2	3	4	5	6	7
1924 ..	$1,818,743,917	$193,096,864 *	$2,011,840,781	89.8	84.3	89.2
1926 ..	2,026,308,190	228,943,137 *	2,255,251,327	100.0	100.0	100.0
1928 ..	2,184,336,638	264,296,923 *	2,448,633,561	107.8	115.4	108.6
1930 ..	2,316,790,384	288,908,502	2,605,698,886	114.3	126.2	115.5
1932 ..	2,174,650,555	282,274,585	2,456,925,140	107.3	123.3	108.9
1934 ..	1,720,105,229	220,028,204	1,940,133,433	84.9	96.1	86.0

* Receipts.
Sources of data (Educational Research Service, National Education Association):
1924—Col. 2: *Research Bulletin* of the National Education Association, Vol. 5, p. 10.
    Col. 3: *Biennial Survey*, 1924, p. 344.
1926—Col. 2–4: *Research Bulletin* of the National Education Association, Vol. 6, p. 269.
1928—Col. 2–4: *Research Bulletin* of the National Education Association, Vol. 8, p. 172.
1930—Col. 2: *Biennial Survey*, 1930, Vol. II, Chapter II, p. 40.
    Col. 3: *Biennial Survey*, 1930, Vol. II, Chapter I, p. 11.
1932—Col. 2–3: *Biennial Survey*, 1932, Preface, p. 11.
1934—Col. 2–3: Received through courtesy of the Statistical Division of the United States Office of Education.

tures for federal governmental enterprises, following 1930, reflect the considered judgment of the American people. It would rather seem to be that this trend was largely the result of the fortuitous circumstance that the costs of services maintained by the Federal Government had behind them an effectively administered modern system of taxes, whereas education was mainly supported through the obsolete general property tax, ineffectively administered by local governments. This circumstance may not have been the sole factor operating to the financial disadvantage of education, but it was undoubtedly a factor in the situation, and an important one.

The material presented in this chapter justifies the conclusion that the United States is economically able to finance an adequate system of public education. The use of this ability, however, depends upon willingness to make choices which will result in an adequate allotment for education among the items composing the total national budget of public and private expenditures. Furthermore, it is not enough that the American people should merely feel a vague desire to finance an adequate system of public education. They must also develop fiscal arrangements which will permit this desire to find practical financial expression under the present economic organization.

CHAPTER II

EARLY STUDIES OF THE RELATIVE ABILITY OF THE STATES TO FINANCE EDUCATION

CHAPTER I dealt with data and factors involved in considering the economic ability of the United States as a whole to finance an adequate program of public education. This chapter and the next offer data indicating the manner in which national ability to support education is distributed among the several states.

The ability of a state to finance schools involves two factors: first, the resources which it possesses as a basis for the financial support of public enterprises of which education is one; and second, the size of its educational task, load, or need as indicated by the number of children to be educated. In short, ability to finance education is defined as resources divided by amount of need.

Until recently the relative ability of the states to support education has been measured by the simple process of dividing wealth, the value of tangible property, by total or school population. In 1905 Commissioner Harris pointed out that the states differed in assessable wealth per capita, and discussed this relationship to variations in school expenditures.[1] When this early method is used to measure ability for the years 1900, 1912, and 1922—the years for which the federal census of wealth makes the data available—wide differences are revealed among the states in regard to wealth per child and relative ability to finance education. The findings are displayed in full in Table 5. Figures III and IV present some of the data in graphic form. Certain conclusions may be based on this evidence. First, it is clear that the states differed substantially as to tangible wealth per child in each of the three years concerned. At the extremes, the range of these differences was approximately 17 to 1. For example, in 1900 Nevada had $17,802 wealth behind each child aged 5–17, whereas Mississippi had but $1,056 wealth per child in this age group. In the same year

[1] William T. Harris, "Some of the Conditions Which Cause Variation in the Rate of School Expenditures in Different Localities," *Proceedings, 1905*, p. 203. National Education Association, Washington, D. C.

TABLE 5. RELATIVE ABILITY OF THE STATES TO FINANCE EDUCATION, 1900, 1912, 1922

Based on Wealth and Number of Children Aged 5-17

State and Geographic Section	Wealth or Value of Tangible Property[1] (Expressed in $1,000)			Number of Children Aged 5-17[2]			Wealth per Child Aged 5-17[3]			Relative Ability to Finance Education[4]		
	1900	1912	1922	1900	1912	1922	1900	1912	1922	1900	1912	1922
1	2	3	4	5	6	7	8	9	10	11	12	13
New England.....	$7,703,420	$11,846,217	$24,269,021	1,262,107	1,529,536	1,766,487	$6,104	$7,745	$13,739	1.50	1.06	1.26
Connecticut.....	1,197,675	2,367,590	5,281,849	208,262	266,340	343,500	5,751	8,890	15,377	1.41	1.22	1.42
Maine............	679,542	1,013,872	1,998,845	160,862	172,381	183,138	4,224	5,882	10,914	1.04	.81	1.00
Massachusetts...	4,324,469	6,330,731	12,878,793	623,211	779,389	906,955	6,939	8,123	14,200	1.71	1.12	1.31
New Hampshire.	464,450	647,180	1,351,745	88,806	96,486	100,866	5,230	6,708	13,401	1.29	.92	1.23
Rhode Island ...	708,291	983,439	1,918,098	100,674	131,462	147,502	7,035	7,481	13,004	1.73	1.03	1.20
Vermont.........	328,993	503,405	839,691	80,298	83,508	84,526	4,097	6,028	9,934	1.01	.83	.91
Middle Atlantic....	24,450,025	47,697,590	77,333,620	3,881,285	4,796,075	5,584,561	6,299	9,945	13,848	1.55	1.37	1.28
New Jersey......	2,721,839	5,895,461	11,743,251	470,741	643,726	808,973	5,782	9,298	14,516	1.42	1.28	1.34
New York.......	12,450,307	25,551,080	36,871,432	1,738,802	2,166,246	2,436,390	7,160	11,795	15,134	1.76	1.62	1.39
Pennsylvania....	9,277,879	16,161,049	28,718,937	1,671,742	1,986,103	2,339,198	5,550	8,137	12,277	1.36	1.12	1.13
East North Central.	19,622,296	39,526,439	68,685,855	4,384,219	4,646,391	5,329,125	4,476	8,507	12,889	1.10	1.17	1.19
Illinois..........	6,957,640	15,458,314	22,171,960	1,319,655	1,432,623	1,610,422	5,272	10,790	13,768	1.30	1.48	1.27
Indiana..........	2,601,541	5,348,769	8,812,871	696,401	684,981	722,596	3,736	7,809	12,196	.92	1.07	1.12
Michigan.........	2,648,973	5,286,824	11,382,054	654,810	712,713	918,367	4,045	7,418	12,394	.99	1.02	1.14
Ohio.............	5,010,472	9,107,791	18,458,563	1,099,466	1,159,173	1,384,436	4,557	7,857	13,333	1.12	1.08	1.23
Wisconsin........	2,403,670	4,324,741	7,860,407	613,387	656,901	693,304	3,915	6,584	11,338	.96	.90	1.04
West North Central	13,753,836	30,537,751	45,909,888	3,044,204	3,179,142	3,296,431	4,518	9,606	13,927	1.11	1.32	1.28
Iowa.............	3,362,480	7,696,633	10,494,918	635,766	584,032	601,385	5,289	13,178	17,451	1.30	1.81	1.61
Kansas	1,928,891	4,558,675	6,234,560	436,692	460,122	467,136	4,417	9,908	13,346	1.09	1.36	1.23
Minnesota........	2,508,594	5,421,413	8,530,864	514,475	581,742	629,537	4,876	9,319	13,551	1.20	1.28	1.25
Missouri.........	3,241,937	5,723,366	9,973,901	915,320	870,456	859,185	3,542	6,575	11,609	.87	.90	1.07
Nebraska.........	1,620,837	3,708,534	5,302,454	322,048	331,209	349,822	5,033	11,197	15,158	1.24	1.54	1.40
North Dakota....	541,459	2,109,347	2,463,653	95,597	178,613	208,180	5,664	11,810	11,834	1.39	1.62	1.09
South Dakota....	549,638	1,319,783	2,909,538	124,306	172,968	181,186	4,422	7,630	16,058	1.09	1.05	1.48
South Atlantic....	5,679,995	13,263,556	27,165,615	3,260,004	3,749,980	4,285,288	1,742	3,537	6,339	.43	.49	.58
Delaware.........	208,811	300,741	617,217	48,982	51,007	53,177	4,263	5,896	11,607	1.05	.81	1.07
Florida...........	354,391	933,325	2,431,235	163,538	230,463	287,239	2,167	4,050	8,464	.53	.56	.78
Georgia..........	928,980	2,146,810	3,867,489	739,330	861,409	959,099	1,257	2,492	4,032	.31	.34	.37
Maryland	1,299,588	2,205,304	3,936,716	331,904	346,064	366,823	3,916	6,373	10,732	.96	.88	.99

	2	3	4	5	6	7	8	9	10	11	12	13
North Carolina	678,504	1,676,812	4,520,052	630,031	731,559	872,279	1,077	2,292	5,182	.26	.48	.31
South Carolina	481,015	1,248,942	2,381,674	464,085	518,910	586,426	1,036	2,407	4,061	.25	.37	.33
Virginia	1,073,209	2,338,988	4,762,633	586,478	649,199	705,698	1,830	3,654	6,749	.45	.62	.50
West Virginia	655,497	2,412,634	4,648,599	295,656	370,369	454,547	2,217	6,514	10,227	.54	.94	.89
East South Central	3,618,668	7,329,325	12,863,781	2,448,913	2,653,169	2,816,464	1,478	2,762	4,567	.36	.42	.38
Alabama	751,829	1,955,975	2,913,467	610,351	700,812	792,515	1,232	2,791	3,676	.30	.34	.38
Kentucky	1,355,439	2,260,837	3,556,843	664,607	682,384	709,985	2,039	3,313	5,010	.50	.46	.45
Mississippi	557,024	1,233,336	2,175,531	527,487	602,856	592,691	1,056	2,046	3,671	.26	.34	.28
Tennessee	954,376	1,879,177	4,217,940	646,468	667,117	721,273	1,476	2,817	5,848	.36	.54	.39
West South Central	4,532,179	13,151,165	19,771,221	2,037,522	2,899,179	3,278,515	2,224	4,536	6,031	.55	.56	.62
Arkansas	601,439	1,713,979	2,587,642	442,984	512,673	581,530	1,358	3,343	4,450	.33	.41	.46
Louisiana	809,615	1,976,282	3,393,690	449,704	538,026	567,549	1,800	3,673	5,980	.44	.55	.50
Oklahoma	810,119	3,111,934	3,986,841	124,788	567,883	669,266	6,492	5,480	5,956	1.60	.55	.75
Texas	2,311,006	6,348,970	9,803,548	1,020,046	1,280,597	1,460,170	2,266	4,958	6,714	.56	.62	.68
Mountain	2,968,576	6,084,297	11,180,982	446,626	703,591	942,505	6,647	8,647	11,863	1.63	1.09	1.19
Arizona	244,209	424,070	1,220,290	31,778	54,528	96,435	7,685	7,777	12,654	1.90	1.17	1.07
Colorado	908,243	2,341,452	3,126,464	133,305	200,541	243,387	6,813	11,177	12,846	1.67	1.18	1.53
Idaho	249,926	523,589	1,387,166	46,309	95,592	130,741	5,397	5,477	10,610	1.33	.98	.75
Montana	574,116	1,059,355	2,079,123	54,162	87,314	151,871	10,600	12,132	13,690	2.61	1.26	1.67
Nevada	160,451	382,012	455,959	9,013	14,887	15,930	17,802	25,661	28,623	4.38	2.64	3.52
New Mexico	244,005	450,310	774,781	59,798	103,442	111,366	4,080	4,353	6,957	1.00	.64	.60
Utah	391,693	755,848	1,457,536	90,161	114,694	141,344	4,344	6,590	10,312	1.07	.95	.90
Wyoming	195,933	247,661	679,663	22,100	32,593	51,431	8,866	7,599	13,215	2.18	1.22	1.04
Pacific	4,496,010	13,358,640	22,862,902	578,879	942,170	1,247,325	7,767	14,179	18,329	1.91	1.69	1.95
California	3,142,937	8,335,878	14,677,855	338,988	500,995	734,993	9,272	16,639	19,970	2.28	1.84	2.28
Oregon	593,515	1,929,466	3,206,783	108,879	160,397	187,820	5,451	12,029	17,074	1.34	1.57	1.65
Washington	759,558	3,093,296	4,978,164	131,012	280,778	324,512	5,798	11,017	15,340	1.43	1.41	1.51
United States	86,825,005	182,794,980	310,042,785	21,343,759	25,099,233	28,546,701	4,068	7,283	10,861	1.00	1.00	1.00

1 Columns 2, 3, and 4 are based on *Estimated National Wealth, 1922* (Department of Commerce, Bureau of the Census) as given in *The Ability of the States to Support Education*, by John K. Norton, pp. 72–75. The figures in columns 2, 3, and 4 represent aggregate wealth less estimated value of federal property. The value of the latter in 1922 for each state was secured from unpublished records made available in the office of the Bureau of the Census, Washington, D. C. Since data as to the value of federal property were not available for the years 1900 and 1912, it was assumed that the percentage of total tangible property in each state owned by the Federal Government in these years was the same as in 1922.

2 Column 5 is from the *Twelfth Census of the United States, 1900*, Vol. II, "Population, Part II," p. 153, Table 10. United States Census Office, Washington, D. C., 1902. Column 6 is from the *Report of the Commissioner of Education for the Year Ending June 30, 1913*, Vol. II, p. 20, Table 2, col. 8. Column 7 is from the *Biennial Survey of Education, 1920–1922*, Vol. II, p. 12, Table 10, col. 5. U. S. Bureau of Education, Washington, D. C., 1925.

3 Wealth per child is obtained by dividing wealth or value of tangible property by number of children aged 5–17. Col. 8 = col. 2 ÷ col. 5; col. 9 = col. 3 ÷ col. 6; and col. 10 = col. 4 ÷ col. 7.

4 Relative ability of the several states to finance education is related to the ability of the United States, which is assigned the value 1.00. For example, in 1900, for the United States as a whole, the average wealth per child aged 5–17 was $4,068. If this amount is assigned the value 1.00, then $5,751 (the average wealth per child in Connecticut) = 1.41. The figures in column 11 are obtained by dividing each of the figures in column 8 by 4,068. The data in column 12 are obtained by dividing each of the figures in column 10 by 10,861. The figures in column 13 are obtained by dividing each of the figures in column 9 by 7,283.

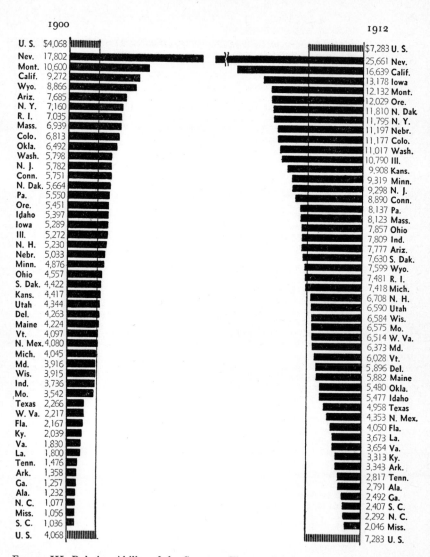

FIGURE III. Relative Ability of the States to Finance Education, 1900 and 1912, as Indicated by Value of Tangible Property per Child, Aged 5–17

The data of this figure are from Table 5

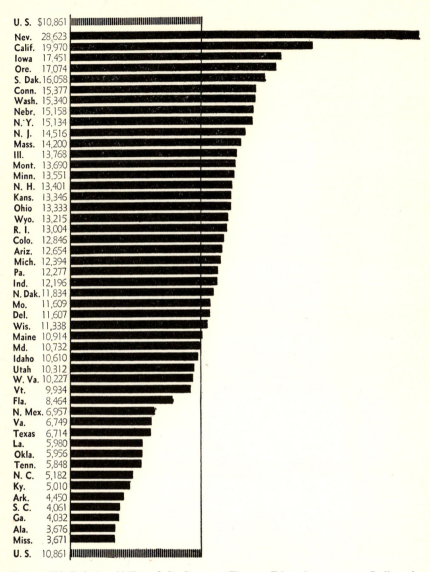

FIGURE IV. Relative Ability of the States to Finance Education, 1922, as Indicated
by Value of Tangible Property per Child, Aged 5–17
The data of this figure are from Table 5

Nevada had nearly 17 times as much wealth per child as Alabama. The wealth per child in twelve rich states in 1922 is compared in Figure V with the wealth per child in twelve poor states. On the average, the twelve rich states had between three and four times as much wealth per child aged 5–17 as did the twelve poor states.

In Figure VI the states are ranked for 1900, 1912, and 1922 in the order of their relative ability to finance education, based on value of tangible property per child aged 5–17. Generally speaking, the states which markedly exceeded the average for the nation as a whole in 1900 continued to do so in 1912 and 1922. Nevada, Montana, California, and New York were near the top in each of the three years. Wyoming, Arizona, and Oklahoma were exceptions to this tendency. The apparent rapid loss in rank of these states probably represents some real loss in ability. Their drop in rank may also be due to failure to subtract all federally owned property from the wealth listed for these states. The method of eliminating federally owned property, as explained in footnote 1 of Table 5, doubtless caused an underestimate of the amount of such property in states like Wyoming, Arizona, and Oklahoma for 1900 and 1912. Hence, these states probably have a higher rank in these years than they should. Nearly all sparsely settled western states, in which a considerable portion of wealth is federally owned, lost substantially in rank between 1900 and 1922. The extent to which this decline is a genuine one in the economic sense, and the extent to which it merely reflects the effect of an underestimate of the value of federally owned property in these states in 1900 and 1912 cannot be decided on the basis of data now available.

Furthermore the states which ranked markedly below the average for the United States as a whole in wealth per child aged 5–17 in 1900 continued to do so in 1912 and 1922. Mississippi, South Carolina, North Carolina, Alabama, Georgia, Arkansas, Tennessee, Louisiana, Virginia, and Kentucky, which were at the bottom of the list of states in wealth per child in 1900, continued to rank among the lowest fourth of the states in 1912 and 1922.

Substantial differences in wealth per child also appear when the states are grouped by sections, as is shown by Table 6. In the Pacific section there was $7,767 of tangible property per child aged 5–17 in 1900 as compared with $1,478 per child in this age group in the East South Central section. These two sections continued to be the wealthiest and the poorest both in 1912 and in 1922. In the latter year, the

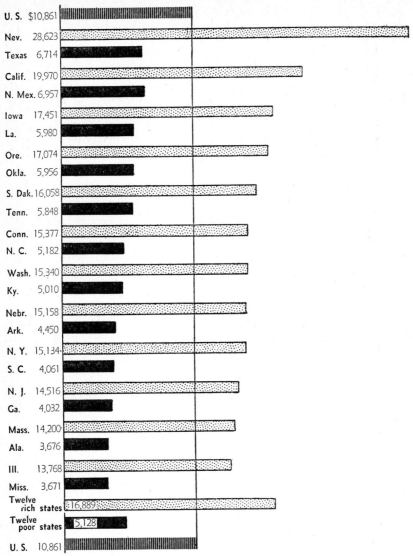

FIGURE V. Comparison of Wealth per Child, Aged 5–17, of Twelve Rich and Twelve
Poor States, 1922
The data of this figure are from Table 5

Pacific states had on the average $18,329 per child as compared with
$4,567 per child in the East South Central states.

Each of the following sections had more wealth per child than the
average for the United States as a whole in each of the three years,

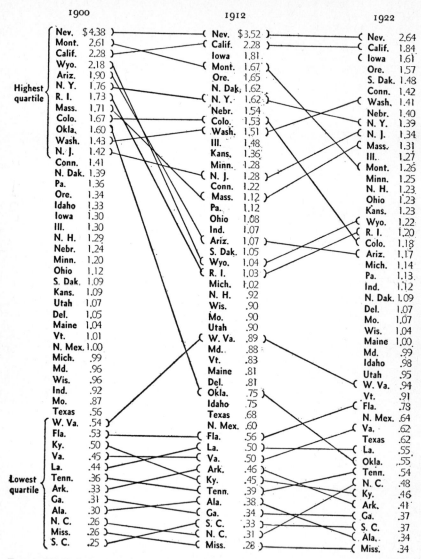

FIGURE VI. Relative Ability of the States to Finance Education, 1900, 1912, and 1922,
Based on Wealth and Number of Children, Aged 5–17 (Ability of U. S. = 1.00
in each year)

The data of this figure are from Table 5

1900, 1912, and 1922: Pacific, Middle Atlantic, West North Central,
New England, Mountain, and East North Central.

Each of the following sections had substantially less wealth per child

TABLE 6. RELATIVE ABILITY OF GEOGRAPHIC SECTIONS TO FINANCE EDUCATION, 1900, 1912, 1922

Based on Wealth and Number of Children Aged 5-17*

1900			1912			1922		
Section	Wealth per Child Aged 5-17	Relative Ability to Support Education	Section	Wealth per Child Aged 5-17	Relative Ability to Support Education	Section	Wealth per Child Aged 5-17	Relative Ability to Support Education
1	2	3	4	5	6	7	8	9
United States	$4,068	1.00	United States	$ 7,263	1.00	United States	$10,830	1.00
Pacific	7,767	1.91	Pacific	14,179	1.95	Pacific	18,329	1.69
Mountain	6,647	1.63	Middle Atlantic	9,945	1.37	West North Central	13,927	1.28
Middle Atlantic	6,299	1.55	West North Central	9,606	1.32	Middle Atlantic	13,848	1.28
New England	6,104	1.50	Mountain	8,647	1.19	New England	13,739	1.26
West North Central	4,518	1.11	East North Central	8,507	1.17	East North Central	12,889	1.19
East North Central	4,476	1.10	New England	7,745	1.06	Mountain	11,863	1.09
West South Central	2,224	.55	West South Central	4,536	.62	South Atlantic	6,339	.58
South Atlantic	1,742	.43	South Atlantic	3,537	.49	West South Central	6,031	.56
East South Central	1,478	.36	East South Central	2,762	.38	East South Central	4,567	.42

* These data are from Table 5.

than the average for the United States as a whole in each of the three years, 1900, 1912, and 1922: East South Central, South Atlantic, and West South Central.

The foregoing data, which measure the relative ability of the states to support education as indicated by the value of tangible property per child aged 5–17 in the three years 1900, 1912, 1922, generally indicate that the states most able to support education in 1900 were also in a favorable position in 1912 and 1922. On the other hand, the states least able to support education in 1900 continued in an unfavorable position in 1912 and 1922. Similar conclusions are suggested when data for the states are grouped by geographic sections.

No figures are given in the present study as to the states' comparative wealth per child for years prior to 1900. An earlier study by one of the authors, however, gives figures which show that differences similar to those cited in this volume existed both in 1880 and in 1890. Taking account of all data available in 1926, at the time of his investigation, Norton concluded:

. . . existing differences in ability to support education are not peculiar to this decade and . . . similar differences will probably be found in the future. There is also some evidence that a state's comparative position, with respect to its ability to support education, is relatively permanent. In the majority of cases it has shown no tendency to fluctuate widely since 1880.[2]

This tendency is shown graphically by Figure VII, which compares wealth per child aged 5–17 in states east of the Mississippi in 1922 and in 1880. As a rule, individual states showed the same differences in ability to support education in the decades preceding 1900 as in the decades following.[3]

The use of value of tangible property as a measure of the financial resources of an area as extensive as a state has many shortcomings. Property has its limitations as a measure of taxpaying ability. The extremely diversified character of present-day economy has given rise to new and highly important forms of income. The physical value of a great industrial plant or business organization is likely to be an inadequate measure of ability to earn profits or to pay taxes.[4] Conse-

[2] John K. Norton, *The Ability of the States to Support Education* p. 70. National Education Association, Washington, D. C., 1926.

[3] *Ibid.*, pp. 55–60.

[4] Henry Pratt Fairchild, "What Is Wealth?" *The Social Frontier*, 3:44–46, November, 1936.

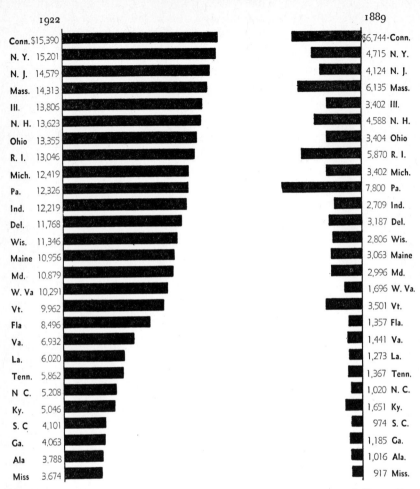

FIGURE VII.[1] Wealth per Child, Aged 5–17, 1922 and 1880 Compared (States East
of the Mississippi)

[1] The data of Figure VII are taken from Estimated National Wealth, 1922, Department of Commerce,
Bureau of the Census, Table 7, pp. 25–27. The data for 1922 in Figure VII are not the same as those in
Table 5, since the latter excluded federally owned wealth in each state

quently, whereas the data thus far given in this study are of some
value as indications of the relative ability of the states to finance education and are presented because of their historical significance, they
involve the increasingly questionable assumption that value of tangible property is a satisfactory measure of a state's financial resources
and ability to raise revenue for the support of a public service such as
education.

The Educational Finance Inquiry[5] in the early 1920's stimulated a series of studies, in which the concepts involved in the measurement of ability on the side both of financial resources and of educational need were critically analyzed. Taking his cue from suggestions of this Inquiry, Norton,[6] in 1926, proposed a combination of tangible wealth and income of a state as a measure of its financial resources. The data presented in Table 7 and Figure VIII are based on his investigation. This evidence reveals substantial differences in the ability of the states to finance education. In 1922 the poorest state had 35 per cent as much ability to support education as did the United States as a whole, whereas the richest state had more than twice the average

TABLE 7. RELATIVE ABILITY OF THE STATES TO FINANCE EDUCATION, 1922

Based on a Combination of Wealth and Income and Number of Children Aged 5–17

State and Geographic Division	Wealth 1922 [1] (In $1,000's)	Average Annual Current Income 1919–1921 [1] (In $1,000's)	Economic Resources— Average Annual Current Income 1919–1921 plus 1/10 of Wealth 1922 [1] (In $1,000's)	Number of Children Aged 5–17 1922 [2]	Economic Resources per Child Aged 5–17 [3]	Relative Ability [4] (U.S.= 1.00)
1	2	3	4	5	6	7
New England ...	$ 24,269,021	$ 5,914,019	$ 8,340,922	1,766,487	$4,722	1.37
Connecticut ..	5,281,849	1,066,910	1,595,095	343,500	4,644	1.34
Maine	1,998,845	460,451	660,336	183,138	3,606	1.04
Massachusetts .	12,878,793	3,392,513	4,680,392	906,955	5,161	1.49
New Hampshire	1,351,745	288,256	423,431	100,866	4,198	1.22
Rhode Island .	1,918,098	503,949	695,759	147,502	4,717	1.37
Vermont	839,691	201,940	285,909	84,526	3,382	.98
Middle Atlantic .	77,333,620	19,123,430	26,856,792	5,584,561	4,809	1.39
New Jersey ...	11,743,251	2,529,034	3,703,359	808,973	4,578	1.33
New York	36,871,432	10,240,721	13,927,864	2,436,390	5,717	1.66
Pennsylvania ..	28,718,937	6,353,675	9,225,569	2,339,198	3,944	1.14
East North Central	68,685,855	15,030,244	21,898,829	5,329,125	4,109	1.19
Illinois	22,171,960	5,215,501	7,432,697	1,610,422	4,615	1.34
Indiana	8,812,871	1,683,432	2,564,719	722,596	3,549	1.03
Michigan	11,382,054	2,586,001	3,724,206	918,367	4,055	1.17
Ohio	18,458,563	3,972,361	5,818,217	1,384,436	4,203	1.22
Wisconsin	7,860,407	1,572,949	2,358,990	693,304	3,403	.99
West North Central	45,909,888	6,979,205	11,570,193	3,296,431	3,510	1.02
Iowa	10,494,918	1,333,796	2,383,288	601,385	3,963	1.15
Kansas	6,234,560	1,019,107	1,642,563	467,136	3,516	1.02

[5] Educational Finance Inquiry Commission Publications; The Macmillan Company, New York, 1923–24. 13 vols.

[6] John K. Norton, *The Ability of the States to Support Education*, National Education Association, Washington, D. C., 1926.

TABLE 7 (Continued)

State and Geographic Division	Wealth 1922 [1] (In $1,000's)	Average Annual Current Income 1919-1921 [1] (In $1,000's)	Economic Resources— Average Annual Current Income 1919-1921 plus 1/10 of Wealth 1922 [1] (In $1,000's)	Number of Children Aged 5-17 1922 [2]	Economic Resources per Child Aged 5-17 [3]	Relative Ability [4] (U.S. = 1.00)
1	2	3	4	5	6	7
Minnesota	$ 8,530,864	$1,354,051	$2,207,137	629,537	$3,506	1.02
Missouri	9,973,901	1,941,856	2,939,246	859,185	3,421	.99
Nebraska	5,302,454	707,772	1,238,017	349,822	3,539	1.02
North Dakota .	2,463,653	289,417	535,782	208,180	2,574	.75
South Dakota .	2,909,538	333,206	624,160	181,186	3,445	1.00
South Atlantic ..	27,165,615	5,726,191	8,442,753	4,285,288	1,970	.57
Delaware	617,217	154,622	216,344	53,177	4,068	1.18
Florida	2,431,235	414,802	657,926	287,239	2,291	.66
Georgia	3,867,489	986,943	1,373,692	959,099	1,432	.41
Maryland	3,936,716	1,025,902	1,419,574	366,823	3,870	1.12
North Carolina	4,520,052	906,437	1,358,442	872,279	1,557	.45
South Carolina	2,381,674	559,053	797,220	586,426	1,359	.39
Virginia	4,762,633	948,905	1,425,168	705,698	2,020	.58
West Virginia .	4,648,599	729,527	1,194,387	454,547	2,628	.76
East South Central	12,863,781	2,994,480	4,280,858	2,816,464	1,520	.44
Alabama	2,913,467	723,445	1,014,792	792,515	1,280	.37
Kentucky	3,556,843	944,486	1,300,170	709,985	1,831	.53
Mississippi	2,175,531	495,946	713,499	592,691	1,204	.35
Tennessee	4,217,940	830,603	1,252,397	721,273	1,736	.50
West South Central	19,771,221	4,754,602	6,731,723	3,278,515	2,053	.59
Arkansas	2,587,642	564,426	823,190	581,530	1,416	.41
Louisiana	3,393,690	762,253	1,101,622	567,549	1,941	.56
Oklahoma	3,986,341	998,170	1,396,804	669,266	2,087	.60
Texas	9,803,548	2,429,753	3,410,107	1,460,170	2,335	.68
Mountain	11,180,982	2,137,196	3,255,295	942,505	3,454	1.00
Arizona	1,220,290	229,209	351,239	96,435	3,642	1.05
Colorado	3,126,464	666,577	979,223	243,387	4,023	1.17
Idaho	1,387,166	252,320	391,037	130,741	2,991	.87
Montana	2,079,123	336,162	544,074	151,871	3,582	1.04
Nevada	455,959	69,987	115,583	15,930	7,256	2.10
New Mexico ..	774,781	166,466	243,944	111,366	2,190	.63
Utah	1,457,536	247,598	393,352	141,344	2,783	.81
Wyoming	679,663	168,877	236,843	51,431	4,605	1.31
Pacific	22,862,802	4,917,764	7,204,044	1,247,325	5,776	1.67
California	14,677,855	3,342,206	4,809,992	734,993	6,544	1.90
Oregon	3,206,783	566,241	886,919	187,820	4,722	1.37
Washington ...	4,978,164	1,009,317	1,507,133	324,512	4,644	1.34
United States ...	310,042,785	67,577,131	98,581,409	28,546,701	3,453	1.00

[1] Figures in columns 2, 3, and 4 are taken from: John K. Norton, *The Ability of the States to Support Education*, pp. 13 and 19, Table 3, cols. 2 and 4, and Table 5, col. 17. National Education Association, Washington, D. C., 1926.

[2] Figures in column 5 are from the *Biennial Survey of Education, 1920-1922*, Vol. II, p. 12, Table 10, col. 5, U. S. Bureau of Education, Washington, D. C., 1925.

[3] Data as to economic resources per child are obtained by dividing average annual current income 1919-1921 plus 1/10 of wealth 1922 by number of children aged 5-17, 1922. Col. 6 = Col. 4 ÷ Col. 5.

[4] Relative ability of the several states to finance education is related to the ability in the United States, which is assigned the value 1.00. The figures in col. 7 are obtained by dividing each of the figures in col. 6 by 3,453.

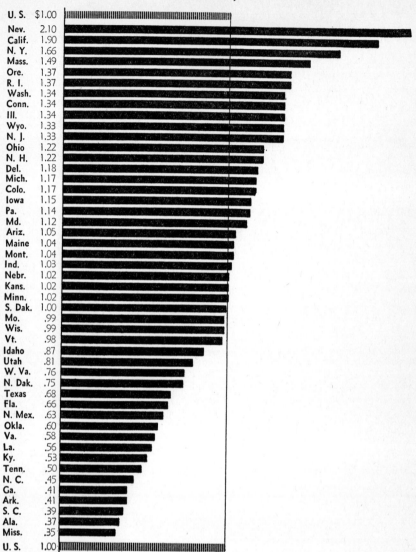

U. S.	$1.00
Nev.	2.10
Calif.	1.90
N. Y.	1.66
Mass.	1.49
Ore.	1.37
R. I.	1.37
Wash.	1.34
Conn.	1.34
Ill.	1.34
Wyo.	1.33
N. J.	1.33
Ohio	1.22
N. H.	1.22
Del.	1.18
Mich.	1.17
Colo.	1.17
Iowa	1.15
Pa.	1.14
Md.	1.12
Ariz.	1.05
Maine	1.04
Mont.	1.04
Ind.	1.03
Nebr.	1.02
Kans.	1.02
Minn.	1.02
S. Dak.	1.00
Mo.	.99
Wis.	.99
Vt.	.98
Idaho	.87
Utah	.81
W. Va.	.76
N. Dak.	.75
Texas	.68
Fla.	.66
N. Mex.	.63
Okla.	.60
Va.	.58
La.	.56
Ky.	.53
Tenn.	.50
N. C.	.45
Ga.	.41
Ark.	.41
S. C.	.39
Ala.	.37
Miss.	.35
U. S.	1.00

FIGURE VIII. Relative Ability of the States to Finance Education, 1922, Based on a Combination of Wealth and Income and Number of Children, Aged 5–17

The data of this figure are from Table 7

ability for the United States. The extreme differences between the richest state and the poorest state were in the ratio of approximately 6 to 1.

When the states are grouped by sections, as in Figure IX, it will be

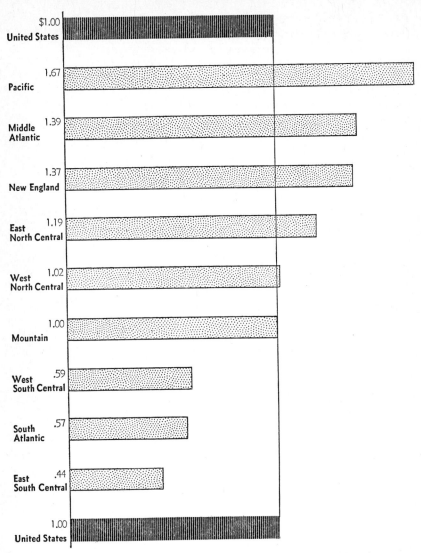

FIGURE IX. Relative Ability of Geographic Sections to Finance Education, 1922, Based on a Combination of Wealth and Income and Number of Children, Aged 5–17
The data of this figure are from Table 7

seen that in 1922 the most favored section, the Pacific states, had nearly four times as much ability to support education as the least favored section, the East South Central states.

When the twelve states with greatest tangible wealth per child aged 5–17 in 1922 (Table 5) are compared with the twelve states with greatest economic resources per child aged 5–17 in that year (average annual current income, 1919–1920, plus one tenth of wealth, 1922— Table 7), one finds that the following nine states are common to both lists: Nevada, California, New York, Massachusetts, Oregon, Washington, Connecticut, Illinois, and New Jersey. There are six states (three in each table) that rank among the first twelve as to ability to finance education in one of the two tables under consideration, but not in the other, namely: Rhode Island, Wyoming, New Hampshire, Iowa, South Dakota, and Nebraska. All but one of these six states, however, are rated as having above-average ability in both tables, the exception being South Dakota.

When the twelve states ranked lowest in ability to support education in Tables 5 and 7 are compared, the following eleven states are common to both tables: Mississippi, Alabama, South Carolina, Georgia, Arkansas, Kentucky, North Carolina, Tennessee, Oklahoma, Louisiana, and Virginia. Two states, Texas and New Mexico, appear in the lowest twelve states in one table but not in the other. Both of these states rank decidedly below average in ability, however, in both tables. There is substantial agreement between the figures of Table 5 and Table 7 as to which states are most able and which least able to support education.

Norton's study was an advance over previous methods of measuring the resources of the states for financing education, since it took account of income, an important indication of economic welfare. In doing so, however, it assumed that each dollar of wealth and income credited to a state is equally available for the support of education. That this may not be true can be easily demonstrated. In the case of income, for example, the upper $900,000 of income enjoyed by an individual with a total income of $1,000,000 represents much greater ability to pay taxes than $900,000 made up of the combined income of 900 individuals with an income of $1,000 each. It is also extremely unlikely that each dollar of tangible wealth represents equivalent ability to pay taxes. Accordingly, more valid measures of ability to finance education were sought. The results of investigations directed to this end are presented in the next chapter.

CHAPTER III

RECENT STUDIES OF THE RELATIVE ABILITY OF THE STATES TO SUPPORT EDUCATION

SEVERAL recent investigations have sought more valid indices of ability to finance education. Measures of taxpaying capacity and of economic resources of the states have been developed. Chism[1] estimated the tax revenue which could have been raised in each of the states through the uniform application of a valid and properly administered tax system for the years 1922–1932 inclusive. The tax system which he employed for this purpose was based, both as to structure and as to rates, on the model system of state and local taxation[2] of a committee of the National Tax Association, supplemented by acceptable tax theory and practice.

Newcomer[3] calculated the yield of a series of selected taxes, rather than the yield of a model tax system, as an index of taxpaying ability. Calculations were made for the years 1920 and 1930. Mort, [4] using the Newcomer calculations as a criterion, developed an index of ability made up of a series of items such as population, value added by manufacture, farm cash income, and net retail sales. Data presented later in this volume develop an index of economic resources based upon ten economic items suggested by the Newcomer investigation.[5]

The researches cited use several approaches in measuring the relative taxable capacities and economic resources of the states. They provide increasingly comprehensive and valid data for studying the ability of the states to finance education.

Paralleling the work designed to provide better measures of the economic or financial resources of the states, Mort has conducted re-

---

[1] Leslie L. Chism, *Economic Ability of States to Finance Public Schools*. Bureau of Publications, Teachers College, Columbia University, 1936.
[2] National Tax Association, *Second Report on a Plan of a Model System of State and Local Taxation*. Wickersham Printing Company, Lancaster, Pa., 1933.
[3] Mabel Newcomer, *An Index of Taxpaying Ability of State and Local Governments*. Bureau of Publications, Teachers College, Columbia University, 1935.
[4] Paul R. Mort, *Federal Support for Public Education*, Chap. VII. Bureau of Publications, Teachers College, Columbia University, 1936.
[5] Mabel Newcomer, *op. cit.*, pp. 74–79.

searches to improve the measurement of the educational task or need of each state. Until recently the two commonly used measures of educational need have been population of school age and average daily attendance. Mort's[6] more valid measure of educational need, based on average daily attendance, takes account of the cost effect of (a) the relative number of children attending at the elementary school level, as opposed to the secondary, (b) the degree of density or sparsity of population, and (c) the variation of prices or cost of living in the several states. The advantage of Mort's measure of need lies in the fact that by using a uniform unit of measurement it permits comparison of the educational task, obligation, or need of the states. "One child" does not mean the same thing in one state as it does in another in terms of the cost of financing a given type of educational opportunity. For example, the cost of educating one child in the fourth year of high school in a sparsely settled section of a state where high prices obtain is more than that of educating one child in the fourth grade of an elementary school in a thickly settled section of a state where low prices obtain. Mort's technique of measuring educational need takes account of these variables and measures the amount of education to be provided in each state, using a unit of uniform financial significance.

The educational responsibilities or need of the states as indicated by the two traditional measures—number of children aged 5–17 and average daily attendance—and as indicated by the more valid measure of educational need recently developed by Mort are compared in Table 8. The percentage of total educational need assigned to each state differs according to which measure is used. For example, Utah, for the period 1922–1932, had 0.50 per cent of all the children in the United States aged 5–17. This state, however, maintains a school system which is considerably above average in attracting and holding its children in public school attendance. It therefore had 0.58 per cent of total school attendance for the nation as a whole for the period 1922–1932. Because of sparsity of population and other factors, taken account of in the Mort index of educational need, school expenditures per child must be somewhat higher in Utah than in the country as a whole to provide an equivalent level of educational opportunity. This is reflected in the 0.60 per cent of the total educational

[6] Paul R. Mort, *State Support for Public Education*. American Council on Education, Washington, D. C., 1933.

need of the nation credited to Utah by the Mort index of educational need. The figures of the last three columns of Table 8 show that if school attendance, rather than the number of children aged 5–17, is used as a basis of measurement, Utah's educational responsibility is increased 16 per cent. Furthermore, if instead of the number of children aged 5–17, Mort's more valid measure is used, Utah's educational need will be found to be 20 per cent greater.

In the case of Rhode Island, a different situation prevails. This state had 0.52 per cent of the nation's total number of children aged 5–17 during the period 1922–1932. Rhode Island, however, has a relatively high percentage of its children in non-public schools. Educational need of this state, as indicated by percentage of total average daily attendance in public schools in the nation, therefore drops to 0.47 per cent. Because of the importance of density of population in decreasing per pupil costs, the educational responsibility of Rhode Island drops to 0.43 per cent, on Mort's measure of educational need.

This technique is particularly pertinent in distinguishing between effective, as opposed to total, expenditures for education. In a state like Wyoming, or even California, a considerable percentage of the total educational budget must go for transportation of pupils, because of sparsity of population. Such expenditures are a part of the total bill for education. They do not directly contribute, however, to the schooling of a child. Rather, they are necessary prerequisites to such schooling. A child gets the same amount of education, other things being equal, whether he arrives at the school building in a school bus or on foot. This factor is not taken account of in comparisons of school expenditures and efficiency such as the original Ayres' Index.[7] It is taken account of in the Mort technique for measuring educational need. As a consequence, the relatively high expenditures per pupil, characteristic of most mountain and western states, are scaled down because of the factor of sparsity of population. The effect is to put all states on the same basis as to adequacy of their expenditures, since sums paid for transportation, which do not directly contribute to the amount of schooling received by a child, are discounted.

Subsequent paragraphs present data as to the relative ability of the states to support education, using the improved techniques described above for measuring taxpaying capacity, economic resources, and educational needs of the states.

[7] Leonard P. Ayres, *An Index Number of State School Systems.* Russell Sage Foundation, Department of Education, New York, 1920.

TABLE 8. COMPARISON OF THE EDUCATIONAL RESPONSIBILITIES OF THE STATES AS INDICATED BY NUMBER OF CHILDREN AGED 5–17, AVERAGE DAILY ATTENDANCE, AND NUMBER OF WEIGHTED UNITS OF EDUCATIONAL NEED

Based on Average for Even-Numbered Years, 1922–1932 *

State	PERCENTAGE			INDEX OF RELATION WITH CHILDREN AGED 5–17 = 1.00		
	Children Aged 5–17	Number in Average Daily Attendance	Units of Educational Need	Children Aged 5–17	Number in Average Daily Attendance	Units of Educational Need
I	2	3	4	5	6	7
Alabama	2.70	2.24	2.11	1.00	.83	.78
Arizona	.37	.32	.37	1.00	.86	1.00
Arkansas	1.94	1.73	1.64	1.00	.89	.85
California	3.04	3.96	4.26	1.00	1.30	1.40
Colorado	.85	.91	1.06	1.00	1.07	1.25
Connecticut ...	1.25	1.29	1.21	1.00	1.03	.97
Delaware	.18	.17	.16	1.00	.94	.89
Florida	1.09	1.21	1.11	1.00	1.11	1.02
Georgia	3.16	2.67	2.54	1.00	.84	.80
Idaho	.45	.47	.53	1.00	1.04	1.18
Illinois	5.62	5.66	5.62	1.00	1.01	1.00
Indiana	2.48	2.88	2.90	1.00	1.16	1.17
Iowa	2.01	2.26	2.48	1.00	1.12	1.23
Kansas	1.56	1.79	2.13	1.00	1.15	1.37
Kentucky	2.41	2.10	2.00	1.00	.87	.83
Louisiana	1.94	1.60	1.49	1.00	.82	.77
Maine	.63	.67	.65	1.00	1.06	1.03
Maryland	1.27	1.10	1.06	1.00	.87	.83
Massachusetts ..	3.18	3.20	3.02	1.00	1.01	.95
Michigan	3.48	3.63	3.53	1.00	1.04	1.01
Minnesota	2.15	2.23	2.36	1.00	1.04	1.10
Mississippi	2.04	2.05	1.93	1.00	1.00	.95
Missouri	2.83	2.91	3.04	1.00	1.03	1.07
Montana	.53	.50	.58	1.00	.94	1.09
Nebraska	1.18	1.32	1.59	1.00	1.12	1.35
Nevada	.06	.07	.08	1.00	1.17	1.33
New Hampshire.	.35	.31	.30	1.00	.89	.86
New Jersey	2.98	3.02	2.69	1.00	1.01	.90
New Mexico ...	.39	.34	.39	1.00	.87	1.00
New York	8.65	8.59	8.42	1.00	.99	.97
North Carolina .	3.15	3.11	2.89	1.00	.99	.92
North Dakota ..	.71	.73	.89	1.00	1.03	1.25
Ohio	4.96	5.33	5.22	1.00	1.07	1.05
Oklahoma	2.33	2.26	2.36	1.00	.97	1.01
Oregon	.67	.80	.94	1.00	1.19	1.40
Pennsylvania ...	8.19	7.83	7.17	1.00	.96	.88
Rhode Island ..	.52	.47	.43	1.00	.90	.83
South Carolina .	1.98	1.72	1.60	1.00	.87	.81
South Dakota ..	.63	.67	.82	1.00	1.06	1.30
Tennessee	2.45	2.33	2.20	1.00	.95	.90

TABLE 8 (*Continued*)

State	PERCENTAGE			INDEX OF RELATION WITH CHILDREN AGED 5–17 = 1.00		
	Children Aged 5–17	Number in Average Daily Attendance	Units of Educational Need	Children Aged 5–17	Number in Average Daily Attendance	Units of Educational Need
1	2	3	4	5	6	7
Texas	5.14	5.06	5.69	1.00	.98	1.11
Utah	.50	.58	.60	1.00	1.16	1.20
Vermont	.28	.28	.29	1.00	1.00	1.04
Virginia	2.38	2.16	2.07	1.00	.91	.87
Washington	1.15	1.31	1.42	1.00	1.14	1.23
West Virginia ..	1.63	1.62	1.50	1.00	.99	.92
Wisconsin	2.37	2.33	2.41	1.00	.98	1.02
Wyoming	.19	.21	.25	1.00	1.11	1.32
	100.00	100.00	100.00			

* Columns 2, 3, and 4 are based on data from Leslie L. Chism, *The Economic Ability of the States to Finance Public Schools*, pp. 144–145, Table 35, cols. 3, 7, and 11. Bureau of Publications, Teachers College, Columbia University, 1936.
Date in columns 6 and 7 are obtained by dividing the figures of column 2 into the figures of columns 3 and 4 respectively.

The data in Table 9, which are based on Chism's researches, show the relative ability of the states to finance education. The amount of tax revenue indicated for each state is the estimated sum which the states could have raised in the six even-numbered years during 1922–1932 through the uniform application of a valid and properly administered tax system. The elements composing this system were a tax on real estate and other tangible property, a personal income tax, a business tax on the net income of both corporate and non-corporate business enterprises, a motor fuel tax, a motor vehicle registration fee, and an inheritance tax. The rates at which the taxes were levied were those which acceptable taxation theory and practice indicated to be reasonable. The amount of tax revenue, indicated in Table 9 as available for financing education, is 31.27 per cent of the total revenue which could have been raised in each state in the six even-numbered years during 1922–1932, if the model tax system described above had been in effect. This percentage is the portion of actual total tax revenue appropriated for the support of public schools by the forty-eight states considered as a whole during the period under consideration.

The tax revenue per child, which could have been raised in the various states applying a modern system of taxes levied at uniform rates, differs substantially. Rich states such as California and New York could have raised annually an average of $98 and $94 respectively per child aged 5–17 if they had employed a model tax system

TABLE 9. RELATIVE ABILITY OF THE STATES TO FINANCE EDUCATION, 1922–1932

Based on Revenue Which Would Have Been Available from a Modern Tax System and Number of Children Aged 5–17

(Total Yield in Six Even-Numbered Years, 1922–1932 Inclusive)[1]

State and Geographic Division	Tax Revenue for Education (In $1,000's)[2]	Number of Children Aged 5–17 [3] (In 1,000's)	Tax Revenue per Child Aged 5–17	Relative Ability[4]
1	2	3	4	5
New England .... $	854,287	11,309	$ 75.54	1.31
Connecticut	186,056	2,276	81.75	1.42
Maine	66,524	1,139	58.41	1.02
Massachusetts	464,989	5,795	80.24	1.40
New Hampshire	43,637	628	69.49	1.21
Rhode Island	67,150	955	70.31	1.22
Vermont	25,931	516	50.25	.87
Middle Atlantic	2,862,447	36,085	79.33	1.38
New Jersey	415,064	5,429	76.45	1.33
New York	1,487,319	15,741	94.49	1.64
Pennsylvania	960,064	14,915	64.37	1.12
East North Central	2,324,012	34,408	67.54	1.18
Illinois	762,194	10,225	74.54	1.30
Indiana	281,414	4,514	62.34	1.08
Michigan	398,691	6,326	63.02	1.10
Ohio	635,890	9,023	70.47	1.23
Wisconsin	245,823	4,320	56.90	.99
West North Central	1,372,766	20,123	68.22	1.19
Iowa	305,871	3,654	83.71	1.46
Kansas	190,342	2,842	66.97	1.17
Minnesota	257,119	3,905	65.84	1.15
Missouri	309,253	5,156	59.98	1.04
Nebraska	159,355	2,142	74.40	1.29
North Dakota	67,612	1,287	52.53	.91
South Dakota	83,214	1,137	73.19	1.27
South Atlantic	868,666	27,022	32.15	.56
Delaware	22,010	332	66.57	1.16
Florida	92,174	1,988	46.37	.81
Georgia	118,382	5,745	20.61	.36
Maryland	132,840	2,305	57.63	1.00
North Carolina	137,930	5,733	24.06	.42
South Carolina	68,154	3,612	18.87	.33
Virginia	147,978	4,338	34.11	.59
West Virginia	149,107	2,969	50.22	.87
East South Central	390,103	17,480	22.32	.39
Alabama	88,495	4,922	17.98	.31
Kentucky	108,001	4,388	24.61	.43
Mississippi	63,685	3,711	17.16	.30
Tennessee	129,922	4,459	29.14	.51
West South Central	639,899	20,660	30.97	.54
Arkansas	76,329	3,532	21.61	.38
Louisiana	100,767	3,538	28.48	.50
Oklahoma	129,866	4,232	30.69	.53
Texas	332,937	9,358	35.58	.62

TABLE 9 (*Continued*)

State and Geographic Division	Tax Revenue for Education (In $1,000's)[2]	Number of Children Aged 5–17 [3] (In 1,000's)	Tax Revenue per Child Aged 5–17	Relative Ability[4]
1	2	3	4	5
Mountain	$ 337,852	6,077	$ 55.60	.97
Arizona	38,091	669	56.94	.99
Colorado	95,212	1,554	61.27	1.07
Idaho	39,817	822	48.44	.84
Montana	60,326	959	62.91	1.09
Nevada	16,284	104	156.58	2.72
New Mexico	24,072	718	33.53	.58
Utah	42,502	908	46.81	.81
Wyoming	21,548	343	62.82	1.09
Pacific	811,854	8,856	91.67	1.59
California	541,705	5,541	97.76	1.70
Oregon	102,188	1,223	83.56	1.45
Washington	167,961	2,092	80.29	1.40
United States	10,461,886	182,020	57.48	1.00

[1] Based on data in Table 35, pp. 144–145, of *The Economic Ability of the States to Finance Public Schools*, by Leslie L. Chism. Bureau of Publications, Teachers College, Columbia University, 1936.
[2] The revenue given in this column is 31.27 per cent of the total yield of a model tax system applied uniformly in each state for the six even-numbered years, 1922 to 1932 inclusive.
[3] The number of children given in this column is the sum of the number, aged 5–17, in each of the six even-numbered years, 1922 to 1932 inclusive.
[4] Relative ability of the several states to finance education is related to the ability of the United States, which is assigned the value 1.00. Data in column 5 are obtained by dividing each of the figures in column 4 by 57.48.

and had allotted 31.27 per cent of total tax revenue to education. Financially poor states such as Mississippi and Alabama could have raised only $17 and $18 respectively per child under similar circumstances. Figure X, based on the data of Table 9, graphically compares the ability of the several states to finance education. The ability of the United States as a whole is given the value 1.00, and the abilities of the various states are related to this base. Seven states—Kentucky, North Carolina, Arkansas, Georgia, South Carolina, Alabama, and Mississippi—have less than half as much ability as the United States as a whole. Eight states—Nevada, California, New York, Iowa, Oregon, Connecticut, Washington, and Massachusetts—have from 172 to 40 per cent more ability than the nation as a whole. Generally speaking, the states which appear most able and least able to support education are the same as those indicated in the previously presented measures of ability in Chapter II.[8] The nine states which fall in the upper quartile as to ability to finance education in both Tables 5 and 7, based upon value of tangible property and a combination of wealth and income respectively, also fall in the first quartile on Figure X.

[8] Another index of the taxpaying ability of the states calculated by Newcomer for one year, 1930, is presented and briefly discussed in the Appendix.

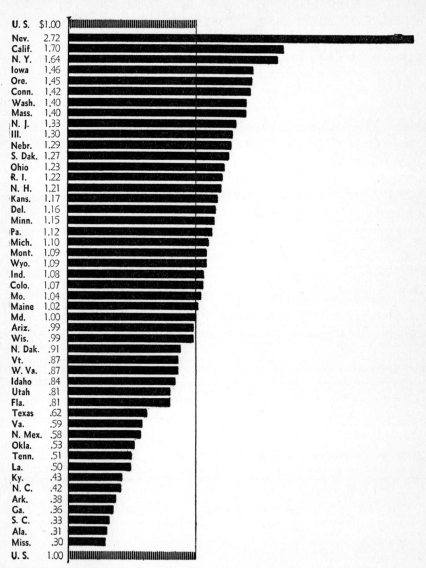

U. S.	$1.00
Nev.	2.72
Calif.	1.70
N. Y.	1.64
Iowa	1.46
Ore.	1.45
Conn.	1.42
Wash.	1.40
Mass.	1.40
N. J.	1.33
Ill.	1.30
Nebr.	1.29
S. Dak.	1.27
Ohio	1.23
R. I.	1.22
N. H.	1.21
Kans.	1.17
Del.	1.16
Minn.	1.15
Pa.	1.12
Mich.	1.10
Mont.	1.09
Wyo.	1.09
Ind.	1.08
Colo.	1.07
Mo.	1.04
Maine	1.02
Md.	1.00
Ariz.	.99
Wis.	.99
N. Dak.	.91
Vt.	.87
W. Va.	.87
Idaho	.84
Utah	.81
Fla.	.81
Texas	.62
Va.	.59
N. Mex.	.58
Okla.	.53
Tenn.	.51
La.	.50
Ky.	.43
N. C.	.42
Ark.	.38
Ga.	.36
S. C.	.33
Ala.	.31
Miss.	.30
U. S.	1.00

FIGURE X. Relative Ability of the States to Finance Education, 1922–1932, Based on Revenue Which Would Have Been Available from a Modern Tax System and Number of Children, Aged 5–17, During the Even-Numbered Years, 1922–1932 Inclusive

The data of this figure are from Table 9

These states are Nevada, California, New York, Oregon, Connecticut, Washington, Massachusetts, New Jersey, and Illinois. The eleven states falling in the lowest quartile in both Table 5 and Table 7 also fall in the lowest quartile of Figure X. These states are Mississippi, Alabama, South Carolina, Georgia, Arkansas, Kentucky, North Carolina, Tennessee, Oklahoma, Louisiana, and Virginia.

The authors of this publication recently completed calculations for a new index of the economic resources of each state. This index was suggested by the Newcomer investigation cited earlier in this chapter. It is based upon the following ten economic items for each state: (1) income reported for federal income tax, (2) farm cash income, (3) value of farm real estate, (4) factory wage earners, (5) value added by manufacture, (6) motor vehicle registrations, (7) production of electric power, (8) bank resources, (9) petroleum and natural gas production, and (10) stock transfers. In the final index these ten items were given equal weight, except that three items—production of electric power, petroleum and natural gas production, and stock transfers— were each given one third the weight of each of the other seven items. This weighting was a purely arbitrary process through which items of less general applicability to all the states were given a reduced weight in determining the final index of economic resources.

The data upon which the new index of economic resources is based are illustrated in Table 10 for the year 1930. The citations at the foot of the table give sources of data used in the development of the index for all years. Tabulations similar to Table 10, not reproduced here because of lack of space, were prepared for each even-numbered year during the period 1920 to 1934 inclusive.

Table 11, based on Table 10, shows the percentage of the national total of each of the ten economic items in each state in 1930. The last column of Table 11 presents the index of economic resources for each state for the year 1930. A similar index was developed for each even-numbered year from 1920 to 1924 inclusive.

Table 12 presents the final indices of the relative ability of the states to finance education, based on the index of weighted economic resources described above, and the Mort technique for measuring educational need cited earlier in this chapter. (Tables A and B in the Appendix give the data upon which Table 12 is based.) Table 12 shows that New England, for example, in 1920 had 1.29 times as much ability to finance the education of its children as did the United

TABLE 10. AMOUNTS (in 1000's) OF EACH OF THE TEN ECONOMIC ITEMS COMPRISING INDEX OF ECONOMIC RESOURCES OF THE STATES, 1930

State	Income Tax Returns[1]	Farm Cash Income[2]	Value of Farm Real Estate[3]	Factory Wage Earners Number[4]	Value Added by Manufacture[5]	Motor Vehicle Registration Number[6]	Production of Electric Power[7] Kilowatt-Hours	Bank Resources[8]	Petroleum and Natural Gas Production Value at Wells[9]	Stock Transfer[10]
1	2	3	4	5	6	7	8	9	10	11
Alabama	$ 44,993	$ 118,035	$ 502,371	102	$ 204,588	277	2,065,000	$ 262,095	..	$ 1
Arizona	19,537	45,520	184,231	8	28,705	111	384,000	75,095	..	..
Arkansas	16,302	86,457	547,829	35	69,354	220	108,000	193,875	$ 18,412	1
California	742,158	567,693	3,419,471	247	1,070,157	2,041	8,948,000	3,350,375	296,909	467
Colorado	66,463	143,169	629,347	29	99,335	309	573,000	241,242	1,560	14
Connecticut	253,277	56,184	227,413	222	638,391	331	1,367,000	1,368,289	..	110
Delaware	47,083	15,665	66,942	20	57,048	56	18,000	166,320	..	12
Florida	69,030	119,285	423,347	57	112,126	328	688,000	211,977	..	..
Georgia	65,403	157,650	577,338	138	238,815	342	937,000	328,835	..	3
Idaho	9,706	91,196	417,250	13	33,720	119	912,000	76,005	..	..
Illinois	963,656	413,459	3,336,049	587	2,334,425	1,638	6,851,000	3,812,535	9,339	2,722
Indiana	144,438	239,891	1,415,542	264	886,848	876	2,943,000	810,320	1,999	1
Iowa	88,505	543,748	4,224,506	71	264,312	778	1,574,000	768,630	..	..
Kansas	60,370	303,138	2,281,102	42	164,750	595	1,014,000	376,027	57,860	..
Kentucky	71,411	121,357	871,449	67	191,022	331	719,000	528,041	15,340	7
Louisiana	68,297	97,489	418,192	72	188,805	275	1,067,000	394,972	34,488	4
Maine	56,082	63,835	194,280	63	145,799	186	731,000	434,728	..	1
Maryland	212,895	62,407	356,170	119	363,143	322	1,889,000	846,456	..	33
Massachusetts	610,965	68,563	261,223	496	1,426,543	846	2,908,000	4,296,033	..	750
Michigan	366,429	208,191	1,160,652	450	1,659,720	1,328	4,270,000	1,963,179	5,392	216
Minnesota	150,301	330,023	2,125,094	92	333,371	733	1,311,000	876,744	..	16
Mississippi	14,371	118,019	568,322	40	76,706	237	62,000	209,420	10	1
Missouri	249,559	262,078	1,796,247	177	632,016	762	1,269,000	1,182,276	72	49
Montana	19,697	82,102	527,610	12	45,602	135	1,320,000	134,594	5,827	..
Nebraska	55,447	344,907	2,495,203	26	99,576	426	575,000	332,569	..	5
Nevada	8,309	12,917	64,111	2	5,950	30	43,000	36,840	..	..
New Hampshire	32,178	26,574	77,356	59	122,317	112	367,000	299,512	..	..
New Jersey	561,626	94,571	297,846	388	1,465,731	853	2,857,000	2,404,862	..	9
New Mexico	11,328	36,846	207,859	4	8,788	84	76,000	39,881	9,493	..
New York	2,747,582	352,568	1,315,905	976	4,193,882	2,308	14,404,000	17,418,434	12,937	41,471
North Carolina	51,299	190,568	844,122	194	657,035	453	2,298,000	353,875	..	4
North Dakota	6,830	131,358	951,226	4	13,779	183	125,000	101,384	..	..
Ohio	538,743	262,613	1,693,031	623	2,232,990	1,759	5,942,000	2,731,039	22,819	90

State	[1]	[2]	[3]	[4]	[5]	[6]	[7]	[8]	[9]	[10]
Rhode Island ..	89,156	9,311	34,506	111	130	207,100	547,000	539,504		29
South Carolina.	17,026	94,116	379,191	98	218	134,350	1,202,000	159,333		8
South Dakota .	11,086	168,696	1,285,154	6	205	20,473	114,000	131,147		29
Tennessee	70,508	111,867	743,222	110	368	267,679	1,037,000	428,744	306,898	
Texas	226,276	442,252	3,597,407	113	1,366	366,621	2,922,000	966,177		3
Utah	21,491	47,932	221,223	13	114	44,458	293,000	157,525		1
Vermont	20,508	47,818	145,935	23	87	60,223	480,000	245,478		4
Virginia	74,390	109,320	855,850	110	376	366,385	1,231,000	540,451		6
Washington ...	99,910	153,927	773,663	93	446	281,117	2,255,000	454,732		36
West Virginia .	54,011	47,995	341,987	75	266	207,241	2,103,000	333,330	37,830	11
Wisconsin	172,168	319,736	1,731,517	224	783	739,970	2,159,000	906,528	23,954	2
Wyoming	8,573	44,224	206,852	6	62	24,558	98,000	54,668		
United States ..	10,392,864	7,869,829	47,872,715	7,658	26,389	25,824,692	95,088,000	57,951,711	1,217,223	46,691

[1] *Income tax returns* equals total personal net income minus the sum of all incomes less than $5,000. The latter were deducted for two reasons. First, the sum of all incomes less than $5,000 in each state is only an estimate. Second, the total of personal net incomes above $5,000 is perhaps a better measure of a state's tax-paying ability. Data for 1930 are from *Statistics of Income for 1930*, pp. 89–138, Table 9. U. S. Treasury Department, Bureau of Internal Revenue, Government Printing Office, Washington, D. C., 1932. Data for the even years 1920–1928 and 1932 and 1934 can be obtained from *Statistics of Income* for these years. Since *Statistics of Income, 1934* had not been published at the time this study was made, 1933 data were used.

[2] *Farm cash income* relates to the value of quantities of crops, live stock and live stock products actually sold off the farms of the state where these were produced. Data for 1930 are from the *Yearbook of Agriculture, 1930*, p. 800, Table 455, U. S. Department of Agriculture, Government Printing Office, 1932. Data for 1924, 1926, and 1928 may be obtained from the *Yearbook of Agriculture, 1930*; data for 1932 and 1934 from *Farm Value, Gross Income, and Cash Income from Farm Production, 1932–1933–1934*, Table I. U. S. Department of Agriculture, Bureau of Agricultural Economics, September, 1935. Since the Department of Agriculture has no data on farm cash income by states earlier than 1924, in making this study the data as to "net current entrepreneurial and property income," 1920, given in Maurice Leven, *Income in the Various States, Its Sources and Distribution, 1919, 1920, and 1921*, National Bureau of Economic Research, 1925, were accepted as an estimate of "farm cash income" for 1920. Data for 1922 were estimated by plotting the data for 1920 and 1924 for each state.

[3] *Value of farm real estate* is the total value of farm land including buildings. Data for 1930 are from *Statistical Abstract of the United States, 1935*, p. 563, Table 537. Department of Commerce, Bureau of Foreign and Domestic Commerce, Government Printing Office, Washington, D. C., 1936. Similar data have been collected in this study: The value of farm real estate in 1922, for example, was found by multiplying per cent increase or decrease in value per acre from 1920 to 1922 (calculated from index numbers of estimated value per acre, 1912–1935, on pp. 6–7, *The Farm Real Estate Situation, 1934*, Circular No. 354, April, 1935. U. S. Department of Agriculture) by the value of farm real estate in 1920 (given in *Statistical Abstract of the United States, 1930*, pp. 624–625). Similarly, data as to the value of farm real estate in 1924 were calculated by multiplying value in 1925 by the per cent increase or decrease in value per acre from 1924 to 1925 (calculated from index numbers, given in circular cited above).

[4] Figures as to *number of factory wage earners* in 1930 were calculated from data given in *Statistical Abstract of the United States, 1935*, pp. 742–746, Table 761. This table presents data for odd-numbered years from 1925 to 1933; 1930 was taken to be the average of 1929 and 1931; 1926, the average of 1925 and 1927; etc. Figures for 1920 can be calculated from data presented in the *Statistical Abstract of the United States, 1922*, pp. 222–230. At the time this study was made, data for calculating number of factory wage earners in 1934 were not available. The figures given for 1933 in *Statistical Abstract of the United States, 1935*, pp. 742–746, were used.

[5] *Value added by manufacture* equals value of products minus cost of materials. Figures for 1930 were based on data from *Statistical Abstract of the United States, 1934*, pp. 724–728, Table 739. This table gives data for 1929 and 1931. By averaging these, data are obtained for 1930. By following this procedure, figures for other even-numbered years can be secured from data presented in volumes of the *Statistical Abstract of the United States*. At the time of this study, data for calculating 1934 figures were not available, so those for 1933 were used.

[6] *Motor vehicle registration* equals number of passenger cars and motor cars combined. Data for 1930 are from the *Statistical Abstract of the United States, 1934*, p. 341, Table 385. Data for each year can be secured from other volumes of this publication.

[7] *Production of electric power* is given in kilowatt-hours. Data for 1930 are from *Statistical Abstract of the United States, 1932*, p. 344, Table 365. Data for other years are presented in other volumes of this publication.

[8] *Bank resources* equals the sum of loans and discounts and investments of all reporting banks, both state and national, in each state. Data for 1930 are from *Annual Report of the Comptroller of the Currency, 1930*, pp. 122–123. Government Printing Office, Washington, D. C. Data for other years are presented in corresponding annual reports.

[9] Data as to *petroleum and natural gas production* represents the sum of the values of these two products at wells where they are produced. Data for 1930 are from *Mineral Resources of the United States, 1930*, Part II, "Non-Metals," pp. 462 and 788. Data for 1926–1928 are found in similar volumes for corresponding years, except that for 1920 no data are available as to value at wells of gas produced. The figures in this study for that year were those given for value at point of consumption. Data for 1932 and 1934 on value of petroleum and natural gas at wells can be found in *Statistical Appendix to Minerals Yearbook, 1933 and 1934*, pp. 105, 308 and 123 and 212 respectively.

[10] *Stock transfer* denotes capital stock transfers, on each $100 of face value or fraction thereof, 2 cents. Data for 1930 are from U. S. Treasury Department, *Annual Report of the Commissioner of Internal Revenue, 1930*, pp. 66–67, Table I. Government Printing Office, Washington, D. C., 1930. Data for other years are presented in similar annual reports.

State	Income Tax Returns	Farm Cash Income	Value of Farm Real Estate	Factory Wage Earners	Value Added by Manufacturing
1	2	3	4	5	6
Alabama	.43	1.50	1.05	1.33	.79
Arizona	.19	.58	.39	.10	.11
Arkansas	.16	1.10	1.14	.46	.27
California	7.14	7.21	7.14	3.23	4.14
Colorado	.64	1.82	1.32	.38	.39
Connecticut	2.44	.71	.48	2.90	2.47
Delaware	.45	.20	.14	.26	.22
Florida	.66	1.52	.88	.74	.43
Georgia	.63	2.00	1.21	1.80	.92
Idaho	.09	1.16	.87	.17	.13
Illinois	9.27	5.25	6.97	7.67	9.04
Indiana	1.39	3.05	2.96	3.45	3.43
Iowa	.85	6.91	8.82	.93	1.02
Kansas	.58	3.85	4.77	.55	.64
Kentucky	.69	1.54	1.82	.87	.74
Louisiana	.66	1.24	.87	.94	.73
Maine	.54	.81	.41	.82	.56
Maryland	2.05	.79	.74	1.55	1.41
Massachusetts	5.88	.87	.55	6.48	5.52
Michigan	3.53	2.65	2.42	5.88	6.43
Minnesota	1.45	4.19	4.44	1.20	1.29
Mississippi	.14	1.50	1.19	.52	.30
Missouri	2.40	3.33	3.75	2.31	2.45
Montana	.19	1.04	1.10	.16	.18
Nebraska	.53	4.38	5.21	.34	.39
Nevada	.08	.16	.13	.03	.02
New Hampshire	.31	.34	.16	.77	.47
New Jersey	5.40	1.20	.63	5.07	5.68
New Mexico	.11	.47	.43	.05	.03
New York	26.44	4.48	2.75	12.74	16.24
North Carolina	.49	2.42	1.76	2.53	2.55
North Dakota	.06	1.67	1.99	.05	.05
Ohio	5.18	3.34	3.54	8.14	8.65
Oklahoma	.86	1.87	2.60	.35	.42
Oregon	.47	1.30	1.32	.70	.61
Pennsylvania	9.28	3.25	2.51	11.70	10.50
Rhode Island	.86	.12	.07	1.45	1.04
South Carolina	.16	1.20	.79	1.28	.52
South Dakota	.11	2.14	2.69	.08	.08
Tennessee	.68	1.42	1.55	1.44	1.04
Texas	2.18	5.62	7.51	1.48	1.42
Utah	.21	.61	.46	.17	.17
Vermont	.20	.61	.30	.30	.23
Virginia	.72	1.39	1.79	1.44	1.42
Washington	.96	1.96	1.62	1.21	1.09
West Virginia	.52	.61	.71	.98	.80
Wisconsin	1.66	4.06	3.62	2.92	2.87
Wyoming	.08	.56	.43	.08	.10
United States	100.00	100.00	100.00	100.00	100.00

[1] The data of this table are obtained by dividing the figures of each of the columns of Table 10 by the totals of the respective columns. For example, according to Table 10, the total income tax returns for

Motor Vehicle Registration	Production of Electric Power	Bank Resources	Petroleum and Natural Gas Production	Stock Transfer	Average of Columns 8, 10, 11	Total of Columns 2, 3, 4, 5, 6, 7, 9, 12	Index of Ability[2]
7	8	9	10	11	12	13	14
1.05	2.17	.45	..	..	.72	7.32	.92
.42	.40	.13	..	..	.13	2.05	.26
.83	.11	.33	1.51	..	.54	4.83	.60
7.73	9.41	5.78	24.39	1.00	11.60	53.97	6.75
1.17	.60	.42	.13	.03	.25	6.39	.80
1.25	1.44	2.36	..	.24	.56	13.17	1.65
.21	.02	.29	..	.03	.02	1.79	.22
1.24	.72	.37	..	..	.24	6.08	.76
1.30	.99	.57	..	.01	.33	8.76	1.09
.45	.96	.13	..	..	.32	3.32	.41
6.21	7.20	6.58	.77	5.83	4.60	55.59	6.95
3.32	3.10	1.40	.16	..	1.09	20.09	2.51
2.95	1.66	1.33	..	..	.55	23.36	2.92
2.26	1.07	.65	4.76	..	1.94	15.24	1.90
1.25	.76	.91	1.26	.02	.68	8.50	1.06
1.04	1.12	.68	2.83	.01	1.32	7.48	.93
.70	.77	.75	..	..	.26	4.85	.61
1.22	1.97	1.46	..	.07	.68	9.90	1.24
3.21	3.06	7.41	..	1.61	1.56	31.48	3.94
5.03	4.49	3.39	.44	.46	1.80	31.13	3.89
2.78	1.38	1.51	..	.03	.47	17.33	2.17
.90	.07	.36	..	..	.02	4.93	.62
2.89	1.33	2.04	.01	.11	.48	19.65	2.46
.51	1.39	.23	.48	..	.62	4.03	.50
1.61	.60	.57	..	.01	.20	13.23	1.65
.11	.05	.06	..	..	.02	.61	.08
.42	.39	.52	..	..	.13	3.12	.39
3.23	3.00	4.15	..	.02	1.01	26.37	3.30
.32	.08	.07	.78	..	.29	1.77	.22
8.75	15.15	30.06	1.06	88.82	35.01	136.47	17.06
1.72	2.42	.61	..	.01	.81	12.89	1.61
.69	.13	.18	..	..	.04	4.73	.59
6.67	6.25	4.71	1.88	.19	2.77	43.00	5.38
2.09	1.01	.66	24.39	..	8.47	17.32	2.16
1.04	1.28	.43	..	..	.43	6.30	.79
6.65	8.28	9.97	4.86	1.31	4.82	58.68	7.34
.52	.58	.93	..	.06	.21	5.20	.65
.83	1.26	.27	..	..	.42	5.47	.68
.78	.12	.23	..	..	.04	6.15	.77
1.39	1.09	.74	..	..	.36	8.62	1.08
5.18	3.07	1.67	25.21	.01	9.43	34.49	4.31
.43	.31	.27	..	..	.10	2.42	.30
.33	.50	.42	..	.01	.18	2.57	.32
1.42	1.29	.93	..	.01	.43	9.54	1.19
1.69	2.37	.79	..	.08	.82	10.14	1.27
1.01	2.21	.58	3.11	.02	1.78	6.99	.87
2.97	2.27	1.56	..	..	.76	20.42	2.55
.23	.10	.09	1.97	..	.69	2.26	.28
100.00	100.00	100.00	100.00	100.00	100.00	800.00	100.00

the whole United States in 1930 were $10,392,864,000; for Alabama they were $44,993,000, or .43 of one per cent of the income tax returns for the country as a whole.
[2] Index of ability is obtained by dividing each figure in column 13 by 8.

WEALTH, CHILDREN, EDUCATION

TABLE 12. RELATIVE ABILITY OF THE STATES TO FINANCE EDUCATION[1]

Based on Index of Weighted Economic Resources per Unit of Educational Need, Even-Numbered Years, 1920–1934

(Ability of the United States = 1.00)

State and Geographic Division	1920	1922	1924	1926	1928	1930	1932	1934	Average 1920–1934
1	2	3	4	5	6	7	8	9	10
New England	1.29	1.36	1.30	1.22	1.26	1.28	1.38	1.37	1.31
Connecticut	1.21	1.27	1.31	1.24	1.33	1.34	1.43	1.46	1.32
Maine	.89	.96	.90	.92	.86	.95	1.03	.98	.94
Massachusetts ...	1.39	1.47	1.38	1.27	1.31	1.30	1.40	1.39	1.36
New Hampshire .	1.25	1.40	1.33	1.13	1.23	1.30	1.47	1.52	1.33
Rhode Island ...	1.64	1.71	1.60	1.47	1.43	1.48	1.61	1.64	1.57
Vermont	1.00	1.03	1.00	1.07	1.07	1.14	1.27	1.15	1.09
Middle Atlantic ...	1.46	1.53	1.51	1.49	1.50	1.49	1.55	1.56	1.51
New Jersey	1.07	1.19	1.17	1.17	1.14	1.19	1.27	1.19	1.17
New York	1.92	2.06	1.98	1.99	2.02	1.97	2.06	2.13	2.02
Pennsylvania	1.06	1.07	1.07	1.03	1.02	1.03	1.03	1.01	1.04
East North Central .	1.11	1.13	1.10	1.10	1.07	1.07	1.00	.97	1.07
Illinois	1.19	1.25	1.27	1.28	1.22	1.22	1.15	1.10	1.21
Indiana	.92	.94	.89	.85	.83	.89	.82	.82	.87
Michigan	1.12	1.21	1.16	1.18	1.10	1.01	.97	.90	1.08
Ohio	1.13	1.06	1.07	1.04	1.05	1.02	.98	.96	1.04
Wisconsin	1.12	1.09	.99	1.02	1.05	1.12	.99	.95	1.04
West North Central.	.96	.93	.95	.95	.95	.98	.94	.90	.95
Iowa	1.29	1.17	1.23	1.26	1.18	1.23	1.15	1.05	1.20
Kansas	.95	.88	.85	.93	.93	.93	.88	.85	.90
Minnesota	.87	.89	.93	.94	.91	.95	.94	.92	.92
Missouri	.78	.80	.82	.81	.82	.85	.87	.86	.83
Nebraska	.99	.94	1.01	.99	1.01	1.11	.99	.99	1.00
North Dakota ...	.70	.70	.84	.74	.82	.69	.71	.66	.73
South Dakota ...	1.27	1.08	.96	.88	.93	.96	.86	.75	.96
South Atlantic	.62	.59	.60	.61	.59	.59	.61	.64	.61
Delaware	1.19	1.13	1.19	1.31	1.35	1.29	1.59	1.59	1.33
Florida	.56	.64	.81	.88	.62	.66	.66	.66	.69
Georgia	.50	.42	.42	.45	.44	.45	.43	.50	.45
Maryland	1.08	1.14	1.09	1.10	1.08	1.15	1.28	1.19	1.14
North Carolina ..	.56	.55	.55	.56	.57	.54	.53	.61	.56
South Carolina ..	.50	.46	.50	.44	.44	.44	.45	.52	.47
Virginia	.59	.58	.57	.57	.57	.58	.61	.62	.59
West Virginia ...	.78	.69	.66	.62	.61	.57	.55	.55	.63
East South Central .	.48	.44	.45	.47	.46	.45	.44	.47	.46
Alabama	.41	.40	.43	.48	.45	.44	.40	.43	.43
Kentucky	.61	.53	.53	.58	.55	.55	.54	.56	.56
Mississippi	.48	.35	.35	.34	.37	.32	.31	.34	.36
Tennessee	.42	.47	.49	.50	.49	.50	.50	.55	.49
West South Central.	.78	.69	.71	.73	.78	.72	.76	.77	.74
Arkansas	.39	.43	.48	.51	.48	.41	.41	.43	.44
Louisiana	.81	.69	.65	.68	.65	.60	.62	.60	.66
Oklahoma	1.04	.98	.95	1.03	1.10	.93	.81	.79	.95
Texas	.80	.66	.70	.68	.76	.75	.87	.90	.77

TABLE 12 *(Continued)*

State and Geographic Division	1920	1922	1924	1926	1928	1930	1932	1934	Average 1920–1934
1	2	3	4	5	6	7	8	9	10
Mountain	.74	.74	.73	.72	.76	.73	.68	.70	.73
Arizona	.64	.63	.67	.63	.71	.63	.55	.55	.63
Colorado	.79	.76	.68	.71	.70	.78	.73	.70	.73
Idaho	.79	.73	.75	.74	.79	.79	.75	.76	.76
Montana	.86	.90	.90	.95	1.02	.88	.82	.87	.90
Nevada	.88	.88	1.00	1.00	.89	1.00	.78	.78	.90
New Mexico	.42	.47	.44	.46	.59	.52	.55	.61	.51
Utah	.48	.47	.47	.48	.50	.50	.48	.46	.48
Wyoming	1.42	1.52	1.52	1.28	1.30	1.04	.96	1.08	1.27
Pacific	1.24	1.31	1.26	1.25	1.25	1.30	1.26	1.25	1.27
California	1.50	1.58	1.49	1.47	1.48	1.50	1.49	1.47	1.50
Oregon	.79	.85	.84	.87	.81	.92	.74	.73	.82
Washington	.93	.88	.86	.84	.85	.89	.89	.89	.88
United States	1.00	1.00	1.00	1.00	1.00	1.00	1.00	1.00	1.00

1 The data of this table are from Tables A and B in Appendix.

States as a whole. This figure is based upon the fact, which may be ascertained by consulting Tables A and B in the Appendix, that New England in 1920 had 7.77 per cent of the economic resources of the nation, according to the weighted index of economic resources (Table A), and 6.04 per cent of the units of educational need of the nation (Tables A and B). Units of educational need refer to Mort's technique of measuring educational need, based upon number of children in average daily attendance in public schools, with corrections for factors described earlier in this chapter, namely, cost effect of: (a) relative number of children attending at the elementary as opposed to the secondary school level, (b) degree of density of population, and (c) price level. The index of ability, 1.29, is obtained by dividing 7.77 by 6.04.

Ability to finance education, according to Table 12, differs substantially in the various states. New York throughout the period 1920 to 1934 had approximately twice as much ability to finance education as did the United States as a whole. California had approximately one and one-half times the ability of the nation as a whole to finance education. A number of states in the East South Central section had less than half the ability of the United States as a whole.

There are some agreements and some disagreements between the indications of Table 12 and Tables 5 and 7, presented earlier in the chapter, as to which states are most able to finance education. Six of the nine states, which appeared in the upper quartile as to ability according to Tables 5 and 7, also are in the first quartile according to the average index of the last column of Table 12. There is less agreement on certain other states. For example, Oregon, Washington, and Nevada ranked above average in ability in Tables 5 and 7. They rank below average in ability in Table 12.

There is substantial agreement, on the other hand, as to which states are least able to finance education. Nine states—Mississippi, Alabama, South Carolina, Georgia, Arkansas, Kentucky, North Carolina, Tennessee, and Virginia—are all in the lowest quartile in Tables 5 and 7, as well as in Table 12. Oklahoma and Louisiana, both in the lowest quartile in Tables 5 and 7, are also below average in ability in Table 12.

Figure XI graphically compares the relative ability of the states to support education in 1934, according to the index of weighted economic resources and the Mort technique of measuring educational need. This figure is based on the data of column 9, Table 12.

Another measure of the relative ability of the states to finance education was developed by Newcomer[9] for the year 1930. It estimates for 1930 the yield of the following six taxes: personal income, real estate, business income, corporation organization, stock transfer, and severance. For reasons discussed on pages 85 ff. of the Appendix, when use is made of the Newcomer Index in this chapter, taxes on corporation organization, petroleum and natural gas, and stock transfers are eliminated. In Table 13, for example, the relative taxpaying ability of the various states, given in column 3, is based upon the estimates of Newcomer as to yields of personal income, real estate, and business income taxes in the several states.

Table 13 indicates the percentage of taxpaying ability of the United States residing in each state in 1930, according to the various methods of measurement described in this chapter. This table also gives for 1930 the percentage of the total educational obligation or need of the United States residing in each state, according to the three measures of educational need previously described. The figures given in column 11 of this table are based on the composite index of economic ability of the states (column 5) and the percentage of units of educational need found in each state (column 8). The figures of column 11 take account of recent research carried on in this field. They probably

[9] Mabel Newcomer, *An Index of the Taxpaying Ability of State and Local Governments,* p. 54. Bureau of Publications, Teachers College, Columbia University, 1935.

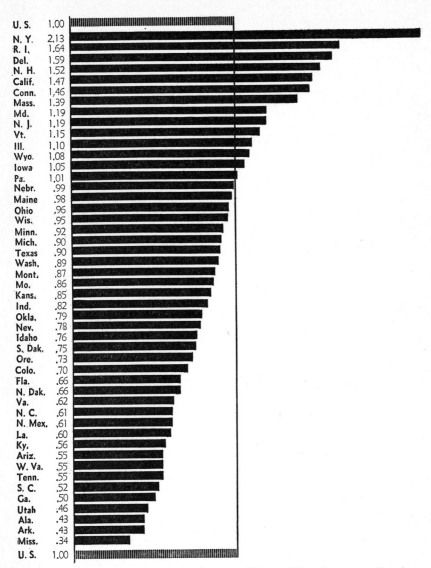

FIGURE XI. Relative Ability of the States to Finance Education, 1934, Based on
Weighted Economic Resources and Units of Educational Need

The data of this figure are from Table 12

TABLE 13. COMPOSITE INDEX OF RELATIVE ABILITY OF THE STATES TO FINANCE EDUCATION, 1930

State and Geographic Division	Percentage of Resources According to				Percentage of Educational Burden According to Number of			Relative Ability to Finance Education Based on Composite Index and		
	Modern Tax System[1] (Chism)	Three Selected Taxes[2] (Newcomer)	Ten Weighted Economic Items[3] (Norton)	Composite Index of Ability[4] (Average of Cols. 2, 3, 4)	Children Aged 5-17[5]	Pupils in Average Daily Attendance[6]	Units of Educational Need[7]	Children Aged 5-17[8]	Pupils in Average Daily Attendance	Units of Educational Need
1	2	3	4	5	6	7	8	9	10	11
New England	8.18	8.24	7.56	7.99	6.25	6.19	5.91	1.28	1.29	1.35
Connecticut	1.80	1.92	1.65	1.79	1.28	1.29	1.23	1.40	1.39	1.46
Maine	.66	.53	.61	.60	.62	.65	.64	.97	.92	.94
Massachusetts	4.42	4.58	3.94	4.30	3.18	3.19	3.02	1.35	1.35	1.42
New Hampshire	.41	.32	.39	.37	.35	.31	.30	1.06	1.19	1.23
Rhode Island	.64	.67	.65	.65	.54	.48	.44	1.20	1.35	1.48
Vermont	.25	.22	.32	.26	.28	.27	.28	.93	.96	.93
Middle Atlantic	27.24	32.83	27.70	29.25	20.10	19.78	18.60	1.46	1.48	1.57
New Jersey	4.12	4.93	3.30	4.11	3.13	3.13	2.78	1.31	1.31	1.48
New York	13.93	19.62	17.06	16.87	8.87	8.81	8.67	1.90	1.91	1.95
Pennsylvania	9.19	8.28	7.34	8.27	8.10	7.84	7.15	1.02	1.05	1.16
East North Central	22.27	21.77	21.28	21.77	19.36	20.09	19.92	1.12	1.08	1.09
Illinois	7.32	7.53	6.95	7.27	5.62	5.68	5.68	1.29	1.28	1.28
Indiana	2.68	2.15	2.51	2.45	2.49	2.81	2.83	.98	.87	.87
Michigan	3.85	4.20	3.89	3.98	3.80	3.99	3.85	1.05	1.00	1.03
Ohio	6.06	5.60	5.38	5.68	5.08	5.38	5.29	1.12	1.06	1.07
Wisconsin	2.36	2.29	2.55	2.40	2.37	2.23	2.27	1.01	1.08	1.06
West North Central	13.13	10.67	12.46	12.09	10.68	11.36	12.73	1.13	1.06	.95
Iowa	2.93	2.26	2.92	2.70	1.95	2.19	2.38	1.38	1.23	1.13
Kansas	1.84	1.47	1.90	1.74	1.51	1.72	2.05	1.15	1.01	.85
Minnesota	2.47	2.01	2.17	2.22	2.09	2.16	2.28	1.06	1.03	.97
Missouri	2.93	2.75	2.46	2.71	2.73	2.72	2.88	.99	1.00	.94
Nebraska	1.53	1.22	1.65	1.47	1.13	1.22	1.48	1.30	1.20	.99
North Dakota	.65	.43	.59	.56	.65	.70	.86	.86	.80	.65
South Dakota	.78	.53	.77	.69	.62	.65	.80	1.11	1.06	.86
South Atlantic	8.19	6.90	7.66	7.58	14.58	13.69	12.93	.52	.55	.59
Delaware	.22	.39	.22	.28	.18	.17	.16	1.56	1.65	1.75
Florida	.85	.90	.76	.84	1.20	1.26	1.16	.70	.67	.72
Georgia	1.12	.76	1.09	.99	2.84	2.54	2.42	.35	.39	.41
Maryland	1.27	1.18	1.24	1.23	1.28	1.11	1.08	.96	1.11	1.14

	Col. 2	Col. 3	Col. 4	Col. 5	Col. 6	Col. 7	Col. 8	Col. 9	Col. 10	Col. 11
North Carolina	1.29	1.10	1.61	1.33	3.27	3.18	2.99	.41	.42	.44
South Carolina	.64	.39	.68	.57	1.88	1.64	1.53	.30	.35	.37
Virginia	1.40	1.12	1.19	1.24	2.28	2.14	2.06	.54	.58	.60
West Virginia	1.40	1.06	.87	1.11	1.65	1.65	1.53	.67	.67	.73
East South Central	3.73	2.99	3.68	3.47	9.33	8.60	8.13	.37	.40	.43
Alabama	.85	.63	.92	.80	2.60	2.23	2.10	.31	.36	.38
Kentucky	1.03	.88	1.06	.99	2.39	2.04	1.94	.41	.49	.51
Mississippi	.61	.44	.62	.56	1.95	2.06	1.93	.29	.27	.29
Tennessee	1.24	1.04	1.08	1.12	2.39	2.27	2.16	.47	.49	.52
West South Central	6.15	5.10	8.00	6.42	11.09	10.50	11.07	.58	.61	.58
Arkansas	.73	.52	.60	.62	1.78	1.56	1.48	.35	.40	.42
Louisiana	.95	.63	.93	.84	1.93	1.65	1.54	.44	.51	.55
Oklahoma	1.27	1.10	2.16	1.51	2.21	2.22	2.32	.68	.68	.65
Texas	3.20	2.85	4.31	3.45	5.17	5.07	5.73	.67	.68	.60
Mountain	3.22	2.93	2.85	3.00	3.18	3.46	3.91	.94	.87	.77
Arizona	.37	.35	.26	.33	.37	.36	.41	.89	.92	.80
Colorado	.91	.83	.80	.85	.83	.90	1.03	1.02	.94	.83
Idaho	.38	.34	.41	.38	.40	.47	.52	.95	.81	.73
Montana	.56	.49	.50	.52	.45	.50	.58	1.16	1.04	.90
Nevada	.16	.14	.08	.13	.06	.07	.08	2.17	1.86	1.63
New Mexico	.24	.19	.22	.22	.40	.36	.42	.55	.61	.52
Utah	.40	.35	.30	.35	.49	.57	.60	.71	.61	.58
Wyoming	.20	.24	.28	.24	.18	.23	.27	1.33	1.04	.89
Pacific	7.89	8.57	8.81	8.42	5.43	6.33	6.80	1.55	1.33	1.24
California	5.31	6.34	6.75	6.13	3.62	4.29	4.51	1.69	1.43	1.36
Oregon	.97	.86	.79	.87	.68	.73	.86	1.28	1.19	1.01
Washington	1.61	1.37	1.27	1.42	1.13	1.31	1.43	1.26	1.08	.99
United States	100.00	100.00	100.00	100.00	100.00	100.00	100.00	1.00	1.00	1.00

[1] The figures in column 2 represent the per cent tax revenue, which would have been available, in the several states is of the total which would have been available for the country as a whole had the tax system, proposed by Chism, been in effect during 1930. See: Leslie L. Chism, *The Economic Ability of the States to Finance Public Schools*, p. 125, Table 28, col. 10. Bureau of Publications, Teachers College, Columbia University, 1936.

[2] The figures of column 3 represent the per cent tax revenue, which would have been available, in the several states is of the total which would have been available for the country as a whole had the personal income, real estate, and business income taxes proposed by Newcomer been in effect in 1930. These figures are based on data in Mabel Newcomer, *An Index of the Taxpaying Ability of State and Local Governments*, p. 54, Table VI, cols. 3, 4, and 5. Bureau of Publications, Teachers College, Columbia University.

[3] Data in column 4 are from Table A.

[4] Figures in column 5 are obtained by averaging those in columns 2, 3, and 4.

[5] Data in column 6 are based on those in *Biennial Survey of Education, 1928–1930*, Vol. II, pp. 44–45, Table 4, col. 3. U. S. Office of Education, Bulletin, 1931, No. 20. Government Printing Office, Washington, D. C., 1932.

[6] Date in column 7 are based on those in *Statistics of State School Systems, 1933–34*, p. 61, Table 10, col. 8. U. S. Office of Education, Bulletin, 1935, No. 2 (Advance Pages), Government Printing Office, Washington, D. C., 1936.

[7] Data in column 8 are from Table A.

[8] Data in column 9 are obtained by dividing those in column 5 by those in column 6; data of column 10, from dividing figures in column 5 by those in column 7; and data of column 11, from dividing figures in column 5 by those in column 8.

constitute the most valid measure of the relative ability of the states to support education which has thus far been made available for any one year. Figure XII presents the data in graphic form.

This chapter has reviewed the results of recent research concerned with the ability of the states to support education. Various approaches to the measurement of the numerator of the ability formula, namely, taxpaying capacity or economic resources, have been presented. Various measures of the size of the educational task or need of each state have also been presented. What are some of the conclusions which seem justified by this evidence?

First, all facts indicate that the states differ substantially in ability to finance education. There is some variation in the range of these differences, according to the methods of measurement employed. The evidence is unanimous, however, that the poorest states must levy taxes at rates at least five times as high as those in the richest states in order to raise a given amount of money per child to be educated.

Do all methods of measuring ability to finance education agree as to which states are poor, which states are rich, and which states are average in ability? There is substantial, although not complete, agreement on this point. The evidence is uniform in indicating that certain states—New York, California, Massachusetts, Connecticut, New Jersey, and Illinois—have substantially greater ability to support education than the nation as a whole. This is true regardless of how the taxpaying ability or economic resources of these states may be measured —whether total value of tangible property, a combination of value of property and total income, revenue obtainable through a modern tax system uniformly applied, or an index based on important economic items is used. It is also true regardless of when the measurement is made, whether at the beginning of the twentieth century or down to date. These are not the only states which have above average ability to finance education, as a study of the various measures of ability will show. Rhode Island, Delaware, Iowa, Michigan, Pennsylvania, and Ohio are somewhat above average in ability according to all measures. In some cases they are distinctly above average, but not according to all measures of ability. The six states named above headed by New York and California are the only states which have distinctly above average ability, irrespective of the methods used in measuring ability and of the time when this measurement is made.

There is even greater unanimity of evidence that certain other

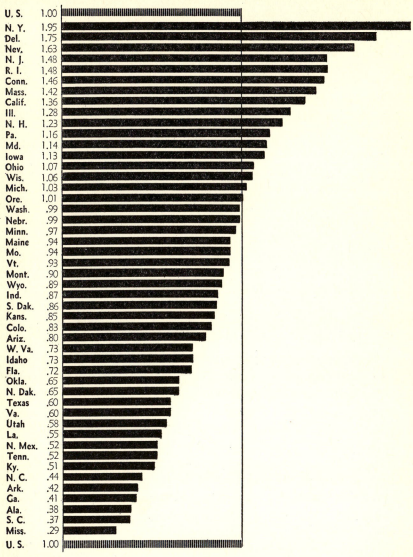

U. S.	1.00	
N. Y.	1.95	
Del.	1.75	
Nev.	1.63	
N. J.	1.48	
R. I.	1.48	
Conn.	1.46	
Mass.	1.42	
Calif.	1.36	
Ill.	1.28	
N. H.	1.23	
Pa.	1.16	
Md.	1.14	
Iowa	1.13	
Ohio	1.07	
Wis.	1.06	
Mich.	1.03	
Ore.	1.01	
Wash.	.99	
Nebr.	.99	
Minn.	.97	
Maine	.94	
Mo.	.94	
Vt.	.93	
Mont.	.90	
Wyo.	.89	
Ind.	.87	
S. Dak.	.86	
Kans.	.85	
Colo.	.83	
Ariz.	.80	
W. Va.	.73	
Idaho	.73	
Fla.	.72	
Okla.	.65	
N. Dak.	.65	
Texas	.60	
Va.	.60	
Utah	.58	
La.	.55	
N. Mex.	.52	
Tenn.	.52	
Ky.	.51	
N. C.	.44	
Ark.	.42	
Ga.	.41	
Ala.	.38	
S. C.	.37	
Miss.	.29	
U. S.	1.00	

FIGURE XII. Relative Ability of the States to Finance Education, 1930, Based on
Composite Index and Units of Educational Need

The data of this figure are from Table 13

states have substantially less than average ability to finance education. These states are Mississippi, Alabama, Georgia, South Carolina, Arkansas, Kentucky, North Carolina, Tennessee, Louisiana, and Virginia. There are other states which rank somewhat below average in ability, such as Utah, New Mexico, West Virginia, Florida, and Texas, regardless of method used in measuring ability to finance education. They are not distinctly below average, however, on all measures of ability. The ten states named above headed by Mississippi and Alabama are distinctly below average in ability to finance education, irrespective of the methods used in measuring ability and the time when this measurement is made.

There are a few states in which the measures of ability to finance education disagree. Nevada, for example, ranks high except when the weighted index of economic resources is used in calculating ability. It is then slightly below average. Oklahoma is below average in ability, regardless of how its economic resources are measured. It differs considerably as to the degree to which it is below average, however, according to the method used in measuring its economic resources. Among other states which differ somewhat in ability to finance education according to the method and time of measurement are Wyoming, Oregon, Utah, Vermont, Washington, and West Virginia.

The evidence presented in this chapter shows clearly that the states differ substantially in ability to finance education. Some states have distinctly above average ability, irrespective of what method is used to measure this ability or the time when the measurement is taken. Other states are distinctly below average in ability, irrespective of method or time of measurement.

How are these differences in ability related to the efforts of the states to finance education? This question will be dealt with in the next chapter.

CHAPTER IV

THE EFFORTS OF THE STATES TO SUPPORT EDUCATION

THE economic or financial ability of the states to support schools is one of the factors which determine the character of educational opportunity maintained by the several states. This factor was dealt with in the preceding chapters. The degree to which a state is willing to allot a portion of its financial resources to education, that is, the effort which it makes to finance schools, is a second factor affecting the character of educational opportunity offered its children. This chapter will deal with the effort made by the several states to support education.

The effort to finance education is defined by Ashby[1] as the relation of the amount expended by a state for schools and its financial resources or ability. More specifically, this concept may be expressed by the simple formula:

$$\text{The Effort of a State to Finance Education} = \frac{\text{Amount Expended for Education}}{\text{Financial Resources}}$$

Amount expended for education refers to current expense. It does not include interest on debt nor outlays for buildings and permanent equipment. The current expenditures of state departments of education and of local public elementary and secondary schools are included. Federal aid and subsidies from educational foundations, since they do not involve effort on the part of the individual state, are subtracted from total current expenditures. Table D in the Appendix, page 86, illustrates for 1934 the method of arriving at the numerator of the effort formula, current expenditures for education.

Table E, on page 88 in the Appendix, gives the expenditures of the states for current expenses of public schools, less funds not raised by the states themselves, for each even-numbered year from 1920 to 1934 inclusive. The amounts given for these years were arrived at by the method illustrated for 1934 in Table D.

[1] Lyle Walter Ashby, *The Efforts of the States to Support Education*, p. 11. National Education Association, Washington, D. C., 1936.

49

Financial resources in the foregoing effort formula refer to the various measures of wealth, income, taxpaying capacity, and economic resources described in the preceding chapters. In this chapter, recently developed measures of financial resources, described in Chapter III, will be used in the estimates of state effort to finance education. These measures of financial resources are based on amounts of revenue obtainable through the uniform application of a modern tax system and relative economic resources as indicated by the weighted index of ten economic items.

Ashby in his pioneer study made available significant data bearing upon the efforts of the states to support education. He employed data of Chism and Newcomer as to the yield of hypothetical tax systems, described in the preceding chapter. The weighted index of economic resources, given in Chapter III, was not available at the time of his study. Ashby's outstanding finding was that, generally speaking, the states with less than average ability make greater effort to finance education than those with more than average ability. This tendency, however, is neither strong nor consistent.[2]

The data of Table 14 permit a comparison between the ability and the effort of the states to finance education. In this table Ashby's method is used in measuring effort, although the data are not taken directly from that study. The data in each case represent an average for the even-numbered years 1922–1932 inclusive. The measure of ability presented is based upon Chism's[3] estimate of potential tax resources and Mort's[4] measure of educational need.[5]

The findings in this table reveal that among the states which are high, low, or average in ability, there may in each group be found states which are high, low, and average in the effort which they make

[2] For those who prefer to measure relationship by the correlation technique, according to Ashby the correlation coefficient for the average of the two factors, ability and effort, for the six even-numbered years, 1922 to 1932, using Chism's data as to relative ability, was: $r = -.31 \pm .09$. The highest correlation coefficient for an individual year was: $r = -.46 \pm .08$, in 1930. The lowest correlation coefficient for an individual year was: $r = -.19 \pm .09$. Negative correlations between ability and effort also exist when the data on ability developed by Newcomer, cited in Chapter III, are used. See: Lyle Walter Ashby, *The Efforts of the States to Support Education*, p.43.

[3] Leslie L. Chism, *The Economic Ability of the States to Finance Public Schools*, Chap. VIII and IX. New York: Bureau of Publications, Teachers College, Columbia University, 1936.

[4] Paul R. Mort, *Federal Support for Public Education*, Chap. IV, "Refinement of Measures of Educational Need Applicable to States." Bureau of Publications, Teachers College, Columbia University, 1936.

[5] For more extensive and specific explanation of sources of data in Table 14, see Chapter III and the footnotes of Table 14.

to support education. For example, New York with 69 per cent more ability to finance education than the country as a whole, ranks second in ability. It makes six per cent less effort to finance education than does the country as a whole, and ranks 29.5 among the states in this respect. California stands well above the average both in ability and in effort. Mississippi with only 32 per cent as much ability as the country as a whole ranks 48 in this respect, but makes 31 per cent more effort to finance schools than the United States as a whole, and ranks 6.5 among the states in effort. Georgia ranks low both in ability and in effort.

Figure XIII graphically presents the relationship between ability and effort. In this figure the bars representing the various states are arranged in their order of ability to support education. Nevada with 1.94 times the ability of the United States as a whole, which is assigned the value 1.00, ranks first. The bar at the right for Nevada shows that this state makes 76 per cent of the effort to support education made by the United States as a whole, which is given the value 1.00. Mississippi, at the bottom with .32 of the ability of the United States as a whole, and with one-sixth of the ability of Nevada, makes an effort of 1.31, which is 31 per cent more than that of the United States as a whole. Seven of the twenty-four states composing the upper half in ability to finance education make an effort equal to or greater than that for the country as a whole, while seventeen of these twenty-four states make less than average effort. Of the twenty-four states lowest in ability to finance schools, sixteen make more than average effort, and eight make less than average effort.

Figures XIV and XV on page 55 permit a comparison of different sections of the country as to ability and effort. The status of the South is particularly interesting. In Figure XIV, which deals with ability, the Southern states, with three exceptions, are shown to be among the lowest fourth of the states. In Figure XV, which is concerned with effort, the Southern states are rather evenly distributed among the various quartiles. In effort made to finance schools, Mississippi, Oklahoma, and New Mexico fall in the highest quartile, and Texas, Alabama, North Carolina, and South Carolina fall among the next to the highest group (second quartile) of twelve states.

The data presented as to the relative ability and effort of the states to finance education clearly show that the poorer states as a whole make somewhat greater effort to provide funds for the support of

TABLE 14. RELATION OF ABILITY AND EFFORT OF THE STATES TO FINANCE EDUCATION, 1922–1932

(Ability = Ratio of number of units of educational need and revenue
available from a modern tax system. Ability of U. S. = 1.00
Effort = Ratio of current expenditures for education and revenue
available from a modern tax system. Effort of U. S. = 1.00)

State	ABILITY: Tax Revenue per Unit of Educational Need[1]	EFFORT: Per Cent of Tax Resources (Chism) Expended for Current Costs of Public Education[2]	INDEX OF ABILITY AND EFFORT United States = 1.00		RANK IN	
			Ability[3]	Effort[4]	Ability[5]	Effort[6]
1	2	3	4	5	6	7
Nevada	$113.87	21.31	1.94	.76	1	48
New York	99.23	26.51	1.69	.94	2	29.5
Rhode Island	87.55	22.96	1.49	.81	3	45
New Jersey	86.82	30.66	1.48	1.09	4	18
Massachusetts	86.54	26.10	1.47	.93	5.5	31.5
Connecticut	86.34	24.45	1.47	.87	5.5	39.5
New Hampshire	82.65	24.03	1.41	.85	7	41
Illinois	76.21	25.61	1.30	.91	8	34.5
Delaware	75.69	25.09	1.29	.89	9	36.5
Pennsylvania	75.27	24.68	1.28	.88	10	38
California	71.40	34.16	1.21	1.21	11	10
Maryland	70.66	22.48	1.20	.80	12	46
Iowa	69.41	26.26	1.18	.93	13	31.5
Ohio	68.45	27.56	1.16	.98	14	25.5
Washington	66.60	27.94	1.13	.99	15	24
Michigan	63.53	35.98	1.08	1.28	16	8
Oregon	61.15	25.96	1.04	.92	17.5	33
Minnesota	61.09	31.71	1.04	1.13	17.5	14
Montana	58.23	33.07	.99	1.17	19	13
Arizona	57.80	33.86	.98	1.20	20	11.5
Wisconsin	57.31	29.97	.97	1.06	22.5	20
South Dakota	57.27	27.41	.97	.97	22.5	27.5
Missouri	57.24	23.11	.97	.82	22.5	44
Maine	57.15	25.17	.97	.89	22.5	36.5
Nebraska	56.15	27.30	.95	.97	25.5	27.5
West Virginia	55.99	26.60	.95	.94	25.5	29.5
Indiana	54.53	33.77	.93	1.20	27	11.5
Vermont	50.75	31.21	.86	1.11	29	16.5
Colorado	50.46	37.82	.86	1.34	29	2.5
Kansas	50.29	31.15	.86	1.11	29	16.5
Wyoming	48.75	45.39	.83	1.61	31	1
Florida	46.58	25.68	.79	.91	32	34.5
North Dakota	42.82	37.17	.73	1.32	33	5
Idaho	42.49	36.83	.72	1.31	34	6.5
Virginia	40.21	22.40	.68	.79	35	47
Utah	39.57	35.46	.67	1.26	36	9
Louisiana	37.95	27.72	.65	.98	37	25.5
New Mexico	34.69	37.87	.59	1.34	38	2.5
Tennessee	33.22	24.38	.56	.87	39.5	39.5
Texas	32.86	28.39	.56	1.01	39.5	23

TABLE 14 (*Continued*)

State	ABILITY: Tax Revenue per Unit of Educational Need[1]	EFFORT: Per Cent of Tax Resources (Chism) Expended for Current Costs of Public Education[2]	INDEX OF ABILITY AND EFFORT United States = 1.00		RANK IN	
			Ability[3]	Effort[4]	Ability[5]	Effort[6]
1	2	3	4	5	6	7
Oklahoma	30.97	37.43	.53	1.33	41	4
Kentucky	30.42	28.77	.52	1.02	42	22
North Carolina	26.80	31.61	.46	1.12	43	15
Georgia	26.18	23.74	.45	.84	44.5	42.5
Arkansas	26.17	23.79	.45	.84	44.5	42.5
South Carolina	23.97	30.41	.41	1.08	46	19
Alabama	23.52	29.58	.40	1.05	47	21
Mississippi	18.56	36.98	.32	1.31	48	6.5
United States	58.80	28.18	1.00	1.00		

[1] Data in column 2 are from Leslie L. Chism, *The Economic Ability of the States to Finance Public Schools*, p. 144, Table 35, col. 4. Bureau of Publications, Teachers College, Columbia University, 1936.
[2] Data in column 3 were obtained by taking the total tax revenue which would have been available had a modern tax system been in effect 1922–1932 (sum of data in cols. 15, 20, 26, 31, 37, and 42 of table in Leslie L. Chism, *The Economic Ability of the States to Finance Public Schools*, pp. 146 to 148) and dividing it into the total expenditures for current expenses of public education less funds not raised by the states themselves during 1922–1932 (sum of cols. 4, 6, 8, 10, 12, and 14).
[3] Data in column 4 were obtained by dividing each figure in column 2 by 58.80.
[4] Data in column 5 were obtained by dividing each figure in column 3 by 28.18.
[5] Obtained by ranking figures in column 4.
[6] Obtained by ranking figures in column 5.

public education than do the richer states. This general conclusion is confirmed when the data of Newcomer in regard to financial resources are used instead of those of Chism.[6] When Newcomer's index of tax resources is used in measuring effort, the superiority of the poorer states as to effort appears to be greater than that indicated by Chism's data. When Chism's and Newcomer's measures of financial resources, based on estimated yields of systems of taxation uniformly applied to the states, are used in calculating the effort of each state, the poorer states appear to make the greater effort.

What is the effect of using the weighted index of economic resources in calculating effort?

Calculations of the relative efforts of the states to finance education, based on current expenditures for education and the weighted index of economic resources, are presented in Table 15. The basis of the calculations of effort given in this table may be found in Table F in the Appendix, page 92. Table 15 reveals interesting figures concerning effort to finance education, both for states and for geographic sections. The New England and Middle Atlantic sections, composed

[6] For a brief discussion and presentation of data as to ability of the states to finance education as developed by Newcomer and Chism, see Chapter III.

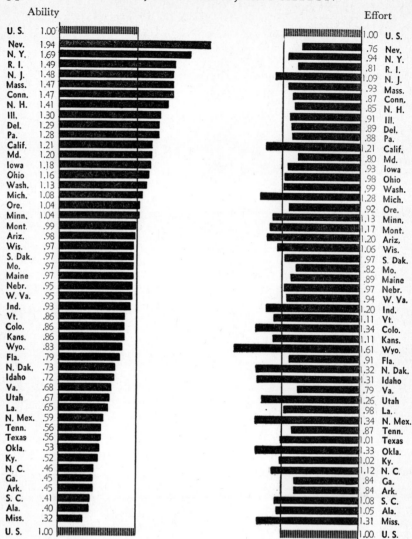

Ability — Effort

	Ability			Effort	
U. S.	1.00			1.00	U. S.
Nev.	1.94			.76	Nev.
N. Y.	1.69			.94	N. Y.
R. I.	1.49			.81	R. I.
N. J.	1.48			1.09	N. J.
Mass.	1.47			.93	Mass.
Conn.	1.47			.87	Conn.
N. H.	1.41			.85	N. H.
Ill.	1.30			.91	Ill.
Del.	1.29			.89	Del.
Pa.	1.28			.88	Pa.
Calif.	1.21			1.21	Calif.
Md.	1.20			.80	Md.
Iowa	1.18			.93	Iowa
Ohio	1.16			.98	Ohio
Wash.	1.13			.99	Wash.
Mich.	1.08			1.28	Mich.
Ore.	1.04			.92	Ore.
Minn.	1.04			1.13	Minn.
Mont.	.99			1.17	Mont.
Ariz.	.98			1.20	Ariz.
Wis.	.97			1.06	Wis.
S. Dak.	.97			.97	S. Dak.
Mo.	.97			.82	Mo.
Maine	.97			.89	Maine
Nebr.	.95			.97	Nebr.
W. Va.	.95			.94	W. Va.
Ind.	.93			1.20	Ind.
Vt.	.86			1.11	Vt.
Colo.	.86			1.34	Colo.
Kans.	.86			1.11	Kans.
Wyo.	.83			1.61	Wyo.
Fla.	.79			.91	Fla.
N. Dak.	.73			1.32	N. Dak.
Idaho	.72			1.31	Idaho
Va.	.68			.79	Va.
Utah	.67			1.26	Utah
La.	.65			.98	La.
N. Mex.	.59			1.34	N. Mex.
Tenn.	.56			.87	Tenn.
Texas	.56			1.01	Texas
Okla.	.53			1.33	Okla.
Ky.	.52			1.02	Ky.
N. C.	.46			1.12	N. C.
Ga.	.45			.84	Ga.
Ark.	.45			.84	Ark.
S. C.	.41			1.08	S. C.
Ala.	.40			1.05	Ala.
Miss.	.32			1.31	Miss.
U. S.	1.00			1.00	U. S.

FIGURE XIII. Relation of Ability and Effort of the States to Finance Education, 1922–1932

Ability = Ratio of Number of Units of Educational Need and Revenue Available from a Modern Tax System
Effort = Ratio of Current Expenditures for Education and Revenue Available from a Modern Tax System

The data of this figure are from Table 14

predominantly of states above average in ability, seldom make as much as average effort during the eight years for which data are presented. The East North Central states, however, make greater than average effort in every year. The same may be said of the Pacific

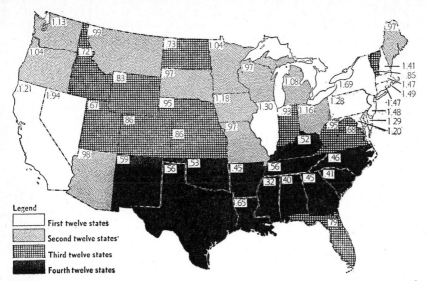

FIGURE XIV. Relative Ability of the States to Finance Education, 1922–1932, Based on Available Tax Resources per Unit of Educational Need (Ability of the U. S. = 1.00)

The data of this figure are from Table 14

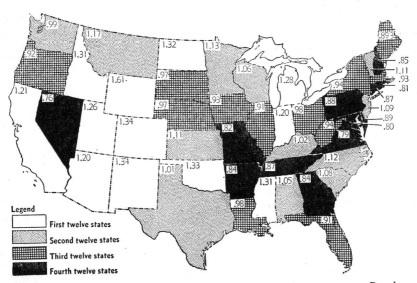

FIGURE XV. Relative Effort of the States to Finance Education, 1922–1932, Based on Percentage of Available Tax Resources Expended for Education (Effort of the U. S. = 1.00)

The data of this figure are from Table 14

WEALTH, CHILDREN, EDUCATION

TABLE 15. RELATIVE EFFORT OF THE STATES TO FINANCE
EDUCATION, 1920–1934[1]

Based on Current Expenditures for Education and Weighted Economic Resources
(Effort of the United States = 1.00)

State and Geographic Division	1920	1922	1924	1926	1928	1930	1932	1934	Average 1920–1934
1	2	3	4	5	6	7	8	9	10
New England	1.03	.93	.98	.99	1.00	.96	.92	.97	.97
Connecticut	1.09	.97	.98	1.00	.97	.93	.94	.88	.97
Maine	1.08	.94	.98	.95	1.02	.85	.82	.83	.93
Massachusetts	1.04	.96	1.03	1.02	1.05	1.03	.97	1.07	1.02
New Hampshire	1.05	.88	.95	1.09	.92	.85	.82	.84	.93
Rhode Island	.74	.68	.75	.78	.83	.83	.82	.88	.79
Vermont	1.25	1.00	.94	.93	.87	.84	.76	.80	.92
Middle Atlantic	.85	.86	.92	.91	.93	.96	.98	1.04	.93
New Jersey	1.35	1.24	1.32	1.34	1.38	1.37	1.37	1.43	1.35
New York	.69	.74	.77	.74	.78	.82	.85	.90	.79
Pennsylvania	1.00	.97	1.06	1.13	1.09	1.08	1.11	1.22	1.08
East North Central ...	1.10	1.12	1.07	1.07	1.10	1.10	1.11	1.09	1.10
Illinois	.98	.92	.93	.94	.96	.97	1.02	1.01	.97
Indiana	1.28	1.59	1.26	1.21	1.35	1.19	1.19	1.10	1.27
Michigan	1.24	1.16	1.19	1.24	1.28	1.36	1.29	1.16	1.24
Ohio	1.13	1.18	1.08	1.09	1.10	1.11	1.07	1.15	1.11
Wisconsin	.99	1.04	1.10	.97	.93	.95	1.03	1.08	1.01
West North Central ...	1.19	1.13	1.10	1.06	1.03	.95	.97	.94	1.05
Iowa	1.05	.93	.98	1.02	.91	.84	.85	.86	.93
Kansas	1.21	1.17	1.11	1.02	1.15	.97	.92	.85	1.05
Minnesota	1.45	1.37	1.42	1.25	1.25	1.17	1.19	1.15	1.28
Missouri	.99	1.00	.99	1.03	.96	.89	.94	1.00	.98
Nebraska	1.22	1.30	.93	.91	.87	.79	.82	.70	.94
North Dakota	1.87	1.43	1.36	1.28	1.18	1.37	1.18	1.11	1.35
South Dakota	1.04	.98	1.04	1.08	.99	.94	1.06	1.00	1.02
South Atlantic	.83	.94	.97	1.00	1.04	1.00	.93	.87	.95
Delaware	.95	1.00	.95	.86	.74	.86	.81	.93	.89
Florida	1.23	1.07	.78	.86	1.49	.96	.95	.95	1.04
Georgia	.68	.80	.85	.90	.87	.85	.91	.81	.83
Maryland	.80	.83	.88	.84	.88	.83	.79	.89	.84
North Carolina	.74	.87	.96	.99	.94	.97	.85	.63	.87
South Carolina	.63	.78	.90	1.07	1.07	1.10	.86	.81	.90
Virginia	.94	1.03	.99	.95	.92	.91	.87	.90	.94
West Virginia	1.01	1.28	1.38	1.56	1.46	1.59	1.53	1.38	1.40
East South Central ...	.80	.91	.95	.99	1.05	1.09	1.09	.96	.98
Alabama	1.00	.93	.94	.89	.96	1.04	1.02	.96	.97
Kentucky	.66	.86	.96	.97	.99	1.02	.98	.94	.92
Mississippi	.68	1.00	.94	1.12	1.29	1.37	1.55	1.02	1.12
Tennessee	.86	.89	.94	1.03	1.02	1.03	1.01	.97	.97
West South Central ...	.81	.87	.80	.79	.69	.80	.78	.73	.78
Arkansas	.88	.76	.74	.81	.84	1.00	.90	.75	.84

TABLE 15 (*Continued*)

State and Geographic Division	1920	1922	1924	1926	1928	1930	1932	1934	Average 1920–1934
I	2	3	4	5	6	7	8	9	10
Louisiana	.87	.99	1.02	.98	.98	.99	.96	.92	.96
Oklahoma	.85	.79	.83	.66	.56	.78	.81	.75	.75
Texas	.75	.91	.74	.83	.67	.74	.72	.68	.76
Mountain	1.75	1.59	1.56	1.48	1.39	1.39	1.42	1.32	1.49
Arizona	2.67	2.10	2.05	1.91	1.56	1.73	1.96	1.70	1.95
Colorado	1.40	1.55	1.74	1.67	1.68	1.44	1.51	1.44	1.55
Idaho	1.60	1.54	1.38	1.26	1.17	1.15	1.13	1.03	1.28
Montana	2.04	1.57	1.37	1.24	1.10	1.26	1.26	1.12	1.37
Nevada	1.86	1.71	1.50	1.50	1.50	1.38	1.71	1.86	1.63
New Mexico	2.17	1.94	1.82	1.67	1.35	1.45	1.38	1.26	1.63
Utah	2.30	2.07	1.96	1.76	1.67	1.63	1.59	1.75	1.84
Wyoming	1.06	.91	.95	1.09	1.10	1.18	1.20	1.00	1.06
Pacific	1.08	1.02	1.01	1.06	1.08	1.02	1.04	1.04	1.04
California	.92	.90	.91	1.00	1.03	.98	1.01	1.05	.98
Oregon	1.16	1.23	1.18	1.12	1.21	1.10	1.09	1.00	1.14
Washington	1.66	1.46	1.39	1.34	1.27	1.20	1.18	1.04	1.32
United States	1.00	1.00	1.00	1.00	1.00	1.00	1.00	1.00	1.00

1 The data of this table are from Table F in the Appendix.

states. The Mountain states, individually and as a group, outrank all other sections of the country in effort made to finance education. The South Atlantic and East South Central sections, except in 1920, seldom rise greatly above, or fall greatly below, average effort. The four states composing the West South Central section constitute the only group which throughout the period puts forth distinctly less than average effort.

Table 16 compares the ability and effort of the states to support education from 1920 to 1934 when the measure of financial resources in the effort formula is the index based on ten weighted economic items, presented in Chapter III. In the table the states are arranged in order of ability for the year 1920, as given in column 1. The figures given for subsequent years permit one to study changes in ability and effort to finance education. Throughout the period 1920–1934, New York State had nearly double the ability of the United States as a whole. Its effort, on the other hand, was 79 per cent of that for the country as a whole. New York, however, made considerably greater effort in the later years. It reached 90 per cent of average effort in 1934, as compared with 69 per cent in 1920. The effect of the finan-

TABLE 16. RELATION OF ABILITY AND EFFORT OF THE STATES TO FINANCE EDUCATION, 1920–1934

Ability = Ratio of Number of Units of Educational Need and Weighted Economic Resources[1]
Effort = Ratio of Current Expenditures for Education and Weighted Economic Resources[2]
Ability and Effort of the United States = 1.00

State	INDEX OF																	
	1920		1922		1924		1926		1928		1930		1932		1934		1920–1934	
	Ability	Effort	Ability	Effort	Ability	Effort	Ability	Effort	Ability	Effort	Ability	Effort	Ability	Effort	Ability	Effort	Ability	Effort
	1	2	3	4	5	6	7	8	9	10	11	12	13	14	15	16	17	18
New York	1.92	.69	2.06	.74	1.98	.77	1.99	.74	2.02	.78	1.97	.82	2.06	.85	2.13	.90	2.02	.79
Rhode Island	1.64	.74	1.71	.68	1.60	.75	1.47	.78	1.43	.83	1.48	.83	1.61	.82	1.64	.88	1.57	.79
California	1.50	.92	1.58	.90	1.49	.91	1.47	1.00	1.48	1.03	1.50	.98	1.49	1.01	1.47	1.05	1.50	.98
Wyoming	1.42	1.06	1.52	.91	1.52	.95	1.28	1.09	1.30	1.10	1.04	1.18	.96	1.20	1.08	1.00	1.27	1.06
Massachusetts	1.39	1.04	1.47	.96	1.38	1.03	1.27	1.02	1.31	1.05	1.30	1.03	1.40	.97	1.39	1.07	1.36	1.02
Iowa	1.29	1.05	1.17	.93	1.23	.98	1.26	1.02	1.18	.91	1.23	.84	1.15	.85	1.05	.86	1.20	.93
South Dakota	1.27	1.04	1.08	.98	.96	1.04	.88	1.08	.93	.99	.96	.94	.86	1.06	.75	1.00	.96	1.02
New Hampshire	1.25	1.05	1.40	.88	1.33	.95	1.13	1.09	1.23	.92	1.30	.85	1.47	.82	1.52	.84	1.33	.93
Connecticut	1.21	1.09	1.27	.97	1.31	.98	1.24	1.00	1.33	.97	1.34	.93	1.43	.94	1.46	.88	1.32	.97
Illinois	1.19	.98	1.25	.92	1.27	.93	1.28	.94	1.22	.96	1.22	.97	1.15	1.02	1.10	1.01	1.21	.97
Delaware	1.19	.95	1.13	1.00	1.19	.95	1.31	.86	1.35	.74	1.29	.86	1.59	.81	1.59	.93	1.33	.89
Ohio	1.13	1.13	1.06	1.18	1.07	1.08	1.04	1.09	1.05	1.10	1.02	1.11	.98	1.07	.96	1.15	1.04	1.11
Michigan	1.12	1.24	1.21	1.16	1.16	1.19	1.18	1.24	1.10	1.28	1.01	1.36	.97	1.29	.90	1.16	1.08	1.24
Wisconsin	1.12	.99	1.09	1.04	.99	1.10	1.02	.97	1.05	.93	1.12	.95	.99	1.03	.95	1.08	1.04	1.01
Maryland	1.08	.80	1.14	.83	1.09	.88	1.10	.84	1.08	.88	1.15	.83	1.28	.79	1.19	.89	1.14	.84
New Jersey	1.07	1.35	1.19	1.24	1.17	1.32	1.17	1.34	1.14	1.38	1.19	1.37	1.27	1.37	1.19	1.43	1.17	1.35
Pennsylvania	1.06	1.00	1.07	.97	1.07	1.06	1.03	1.13	1.02	1.09	1.03	1.08	1.03	1.11	1.01	1.22	1.04	1.08
Oklahoma	1.04	.85	.98	.79	.95	.83	1.03	.66	1.10	.56	.93	.78	.81	.81	.79	.75	.95	.75
Vermont	1.00	1.25	1.03	1.00	1.00	.94	1.07	.93	1.07	.87	1.14	.84	1.27	.76	1.15	.80	1.09	.92
Nebraska	.99	1.22	.94	1.30	1.01	.93	.99	.91	1.01	.87	1.11	.79	.99	.82	.99	.70	1.00	.94

58

	1	2	3	4	5	6	7	8	9	10	11	12	13	14	15	16	17	18
Kansas	.95	1.21	.88	1.17	.85	1.11	.93	1.02	.93	1.15	.93	.97	.88	.92	.85	.85	.90	1.05
Washington	.93	1.66	.88	1.46	.86	1.39	.84	1.34	.85	1.27	.89	1.20	.89	1.18	.89	1.04	.88	1.32
Indiana	.92	1.28	.94	1.59	.89	1.26	.85	1.21	.83	1.35	.89	1.19	.82	1.19	.82	1.10	.87	1.27
Maine	.89	1.08	.96	.94	.90	.98	.92	.95	.86	1.02	.95	.85	1.03	.82	.98	.83	.94	.93
Nevada	.88	1.86	.88	1.71	1.00	1.50	1.00	1.50	.89	1.50	1.00	1.38	.78	1.71	.78	1.86	.90	1.63
Minnesota	.87	1.45	.89	1.37	.93	1.42	.94	1.25	.91	1.25	.95	1.17	.94	1.19	.92	1.15	.92	1.28
Montana	.86	2.04	.90	1.57	.90	1.37	.95	1.24	1.02	1.10	.88	1.26	.82	1.26	.87	1.12	.90	1.37
Louisiana	.81	.87	.69	.99	.65	1.02	.68	.98	.65	.98	.60	.99	.62	.96	.60	.92	.66	.96
Texas	.80	.75	.66	.91	.70	.74	.68	.83	.76	.67	.75	.74	.87	.72	.90	.68	.77	.76
Colorado	.79	1.40	.76	1.55	.68	1.74	.71	1.67	.70	1.68	.78	1.44	.73	1.51	.70	1.49	.73	1.55
Idaho	.79	1.60	.73	1.54	.75	1.38	.74	1.26	.79	1.17	.79	1.15	.75	1.13	.76	1.03	.76	1.28
Oregon	.79	1.16	.85	1.23	.84	1.18	.87	1.12	.81	1.21	.92	1.10	.74	1.09	.73	1.00	.82	1.14
Missouri	.78	.99	.80	1.00	.82	.99	.81	1.03	.82	.96	.85	.89	.87	.94	.86	1.00	.83	.98
West Virginia	.78	1.01	.69	1.28	.66	1.38	.62	1.56	.61	1.46	.57	1.59	.55	1.53	.55	1.38	.63	1.40
North Dakota	.70	.87	.70	1.43	.84	1.36	.74	1.28	.82	1.18	.69	1.37	.71	1.18	.66	1.11	.73	1.35
Arizona	.64	2.67	.63	2.10	.67	2.05	.63	1.91	.71	1.56	.63	1.73	.55	1.96	.55	1.70	.63	1.95
Kentucky	.61	.66	.53	.86	.53	.96	.58	.97	.55	.99	.55	1.02	.54	.98	.56	.94	.56	.92
Virginia	.59	.94	.58	1.03	.57	.99	.57	.95	.57	.92	.58	.91	.61	.87	.62	.90	.59	.94
North Carolina	.56	.74	.55	.87	.55	.96	.56	.99	.57	.94	.54	.97	.53	.85	.61	.63	.56	.87
Florida	.56	1.23	.64	1.07	.81	.78	.88	.86	.62	1.49	.66	.96	.66	.95	.66	.95	.69	1.04
South Carolina	.50	.63	.46	.78	.50	.90	.44	1.07	.44	1.07	.44	1.10	.45	.86	.52	.81	.47	.90
Georgia	.50	.68	.42	.80	.42	.85	.45	.90	.44	.87	.45	.85	.43	.91	.50	.81	.45	.83
Mississippi	.48	.68	.35	1.00	.35	.94	.34	1.12	.37	1.29	.32	1.37	.31	1.55	.34	1.02	.36	1.12
Utah	.48	2.30	.47	2.07	.47	1.96	.48	1.76	.50	1.67	.50	1.63	.48	1.59	.46	1.75	.48	1.84
New Mexico	.42	2.17	.47	1.94	.44	1.82	.46	1.67	.59	1.35	.52	1.45	.55	1.38	.61	1.26	.51	1.63
Alabama	.41	1.00	.40	.93	.43	.94	.48	.89	.45	.96	.44	1.04	.40	1.02	.43	.96	.43	.97
Tennessee	.42	.86	.47	.89	.49	.94	.50	1.03	.49	1.02	.50	1.03	.50	1.01	.55	.97	.49	.97
Arkansas	.39	.88	.43	.76	.48	.74	.51	.81	.48	.84	.41	1.00	.41	.90	.43	.75	.44	.84
United States	1.00	1.00	1.00	1.00	1.00	1.00	1.00	1.00	1.00	1.00	1.00	1.00	1.00	1.00	1.00	1.00	1.00	1.00

[1] Data as to ability, columns 1, 3, 5, 7, 9, 11, 13, 15, and 17, are from Table A.
[2] Data as to effort, columns 2, 4, 6, 8, 10, 12, 14, 16, and 18, are from Table F.

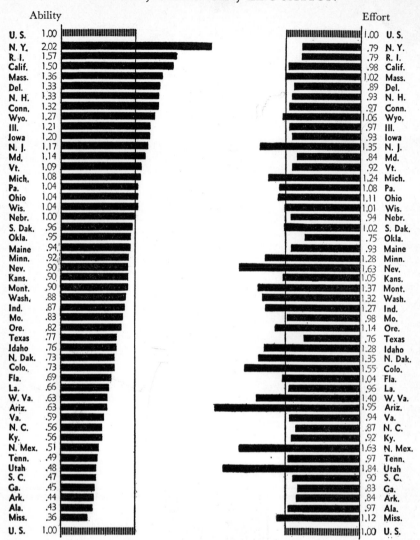

FIGURE XVI. Relation of Ability and Effort of the States to Finance Education, 1920–1934

Ability = Ratio of Number of Units of Educational Need and Weighted Economic Resources
Effort = Ratio of Current Expenditures for Education and Weighted Economic Resources
The data of this figure are from Table 16

cial equalization plan, developed in this state during this period, is doubtless one of the factors involved in this trend. The status of Iowa as to ability and effort is also interesting. It stood above average in both in 1920, but following this year it dropped in effort relative to the trend for the country as a whole. Mississippi had considerably less

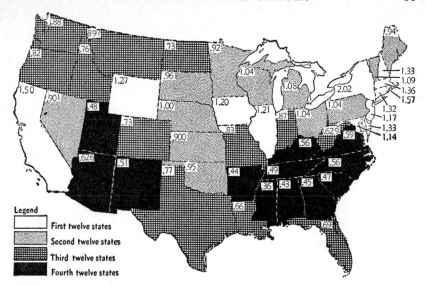

FIGURE XVII. Relative Ability of the States to Finance Education, 1920–1934, Based on Weighted Economic Resources per Unit of Educational Need (Ability of U. S. =1.00)

The data of this figure are from Table 16

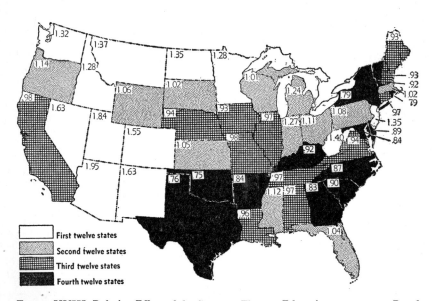

FIGURE XVIII. Relative Effort of the States to Finance Education, 1920–1934, Based on Ratio of Current Expenditures for Education and Weighted Economic Resources (Effort of U. S. = 1.00)

The data of this figure are from Table 16

TABLE 17. COMPARISON OF RELATIVE ABILITIES AND EFFORTS OF THE STATES
TO FINANCE EDUCATION, 1922–1932

Based on Weighted Economic Resources per Unit of Educational Need
and Revenue Available from a Modern Tax System

State	Relative Ability to Finance Education Based on:		Relative Efforts to Finance Education Based on:		Rank Based on Data in Columns			
	Weighted Economic Resources per Unit of Educational Need[1]	Revenue Available from Modern Tax System per Unit of Educational Need[2]	Ratio of Current Expenditures for Education and Weighted Economic Resources[3]	Ratio of Current Expenditures for Education and Revenue Available from Modern Tax System[4]	2	3	4	5
1	2	3	4	5	6	7	8	9
New York	2.01	1.69	.78	.94	1	2	45.5	29.5
Rhode Island	1.55	1.49	.78	.81	2	3	45.5	45
California	1.50	1.21	.97	1.21	3	11	27.5	10
Massachusetts	1.36	1.47	1.01	.93	4	5.5	23	31.5
Connecticut	1.32	1.47	.96	.87	5	5.5	31	39.5
New Hampshire	1.31	1.41	.92	.85	6.5	7	38.5	41
Delaware	1.31	1.29	.87	.89	6.5	9	41	36.5
Wyoming	1.27	.83	1.07	1.61	8	31	18.5	1
Illinois	1.23	1.30	.96	.91	9	8	31	34.5
Iowa	1.20	1.18	.92	.93	10	13	38.5	31.5
New Jersey	1.19	1.48	1.34	1.09	11	4	7	18
Maryland	1.14	1.20	.84	.80	12	12	43.5	46
Michigan	1.11	1.08	1.25	1.28	13	16	14	8
Vermont	1.10	.86	.89	1.11	14	29	40	16.5
Wisconsin	1.04	.97	1.00	1.06	16	22.5	24	20
Pennsylvania	1.04	1.28	1.07	.88	16	10	18.5	38
Ohio	1.04	1.16	1.11	.98	16	14	17	25.5
Nebraska	1.01	.95	.94	.97	18	25.5	35	27.5
Oklahoma	.97	.53	.74	1.33	19	41	48	4
South Dakota	.95	.97	1.02	.97	20	22.5	21.5	27.5

	2	3	4	5	6	7	8	9
Maine	.94	.97	.93	.89	21	22.5	36.5	36.5
Nevada	.93	1.94	1.55	.76	22.5	1	5	48
Minnesota	.93	1.04	1.28	1.13	22.5	17.5	12	14
Montana	.91	.99	1.30	1.17	24	19	10	13
Kansas	.90	.86	1.06	1.11	25	29	20	16.5
Indiana	.87	.93	1.30	1.20	26.5	27	10	11.5
Washington	.87	1.13	1.31	.99	26.5	15	8	24
Oregon	.84	1.04	1.16	.92	28	17.5	16	33
Missouri	.83	.97	.97	.82	29	22.5	27.5	44
Idaho	.76	.72	1.27	1.31	30	34	13	6.5
North Dakota	.75	.73	1.30	1.32	31	33	10	5
Texas	.74	.56	.77	1.01	32	39.5	47	23
Colorado	.73	.86	1.60	1.34	33	29	3.5	2.5
Florida	.71	.79	1.02	.91	34	32	21.5	34.5
Louisiana	.65	.65	.99	.98	35	37	25.5	25.5
Arizona	.64	.98	1.89	1.20	36	20	1	11.5
West Virginia	.62	.95	1.47	.94	37	25.5	6	29.5
Virginia	.58	.68	.95	.79	38	35	34	47
Kentucky	.55	.52	.96	1.02	39.5	42	31	22
North Carolina	.55	.46	.93	1.12	39.5	43	36.5	15
New Mexico	.51	.59	1.60	1.34	41	38	3.5	2.5
Tennessee	.49	.56	.99	.87	42	39.5	25.5	39.5
Utah	.48	.67	1.78	1.26	43	36	2	9
South Carolina	.46	.41	.96	1.08	44	46	31	19
Arkansas	.45	.45	.84	.84	45	44.5	43.5	42.5
Georgia	.44	.45	.86	.84	46	44.5	42	42.5
Alabama	.43	.40	.96	1.05	47	47	31	21
Mississippi	.34	.32	1.21	1.31	48	48	15	6.5
United States	1.00	1.00	1.00	1.00				

1 Data in column 2 are obtained by averaging figures in columns 3–8 of Table 16.
2 Data in column 3 are from Table 14, column 4.
3 Data in column 4 are the average of the figures in columns 3–8 of Table 15.
4 Data in column 5 are from Table 14, column 5.

than average ability in every year, but made greater than average effort except in 1920 and 1924. Georgia, like Mississippi, is very low in ability, but in no year rises to as much as average in effort. Indiana is always somewhat below average in ability, and somewhat above average in effort.

Figure XVI graphically compares the ability and effort of the states, as set forth in columns 17 and 18 of Table 16. The conclusion which may be drawn from this figure is similar to that suggested by Figure XIII, namely, that there is a slight negative correlation between the ability and the effort of the states to finance education.

The relative ability and effort of the states to finance education are shown in Figures XVII and XVIII in a form which permits comparison of geographic sections.

It should be kept in mind that the foregoing comments on the ability and effort of the states to finance education involve the use of the weighted index of economic items as the measure of financial resources in both the ability and the effort formula. What difference does the use of Chism's measure of financial resources, namely, yield of a modern tax system uniformly applied, make in a state's standing in ability and effort? Table 17 answers this question. The degree of correspondence of the ability of the states, when the different measures of financial resources cited above are used, is revealed in columns 2 and 3. Generally speaking, there is a considerable degree of correspondence. There is also a reasonable degree of correspondence as to rank in effort.

The evidence presented in this and the previous chapter justifies certain major conclusions. The wide differences among the states in relative ability to finance education are not offset by substantially greater effort on the part of the poorer states. The states with least ability to finance education really do make slightly greater effort than those with most ability. The difference in the adequacy of financial support provided education in different states, therefore, must be due to differences in ability rather than to differences in effort. Insufficient financial support for education in the poorer states cannot be charged to lack of effort, since these states as a group make greater effort to finance schools than do the richer states.

What is the relative adequacy of financial support provided for schools in the different states? This question will be dealt with in the next chapter.

CHAPTER V

ADEQUACY OF FINANCIAL SUPPORT AS RELATED TO ABILITY AND EFFORT

THE preceding chapters have presented various measures of the relative ability and effort of the states to finance education. What is the relation of these factors to the adequacy of school support? More specifically, does the level of financial support enjoyed by the schools of a state depend primarily upon its ability, or upon the effort it makes, to finance education?

Adequacy of financial support for education is defined as expenditures for current expense per unit of educational need. In this formula for adequacy, expenditures for current expense are calculated as described in Chapter IV. The units of educational need are the number of children attending school, weighted for the factors used in the Mort technique, described in Chapter III.

In Table 18 are shown expenditures for current expense per thousand units of educational need for even-numbered years from 1920 to 1934 inclusive. The meaning of these figures may be simplified by stating that the $49,337 given for Connecticut for 1920 means essentially that this state expended $49.34 per elementary school pupil in 1920. The most important modification of this simplified statement is that although the number of elementary school pupils is taken as the basis of calculation, certain corrections are made by the Mort technique of calculating educational need. The factors taken account of are: (a) ratio of elementary to secondary school pupils, (b) degree of sparsity or density of population, and (c) price level or cost of living.

The marked differences in the amounts of money that the various states expend per unit of educational need are shown in column 11 of Table 18. The rich states generally expend considerably larger amounts per pupil than do the poor states.

Is ability or effort primarily responsible for the wide range in adequacy of financial support revealed in Table 18? The data of Table 19 answer this question. Column 2 of this table indicates the ability of the states to finance education during the period 1922 to 1932. The

TABLE 18. EXPENDITURES FOR CURRENT EXPENSES PER THOUSAND UNITS OF EDUCATIONAL NEED BY YEARS, 1920–1934

State and Geographic Division	1920	1922	1924	1926	1928	1930	1932	1934	Average 1920–1934	Index Column 10 U.S.=1.00
1	2	3	4	5	6	7	8	9	10	11
New England	$49,896	$59,056	$63,109	$63,510	$70,630	$71,516	$68,284	$58,616	$63,077	1.27
Connecticut	49,337	56,821	63,313	65,097	71,816	72,932	72,484	56,171	63,496	1.28
Maine	36,123	42,392	44,021	46,381	49,041	47,930	45,930	36,056	43,484	.87
Massachusetts	54,189	65,817	69,973	67,751	77,575	77,946	72,865	65,730	68,981	1.39
New Hampshire	49,542	57,114	62,329	64,402	65,382	65,570	65,245	55,263	60,606	1.22
Rhode Island	46,063	54,883	57,889	60,847	66,588	71,445	70,673	62,980	61,421	1.23
Vermont	46,838	47,729	45,686	52,272	52,214	55,954	50,045	39,625	48,795	.98
Middle Atlantic	46,485	61,379	67,802	71,458	78,343	82,950	81,451	71,669	70,192	1.41
New Jersey	54,242	69,126	76,085	81,957	88,870	94,866	93,745	75,385	79,285	1.59
New York	49,656	70,850	75,476	77,092	87,992	94,168	93,775	84,716	79,216	1.59
Pennsylvania	39,942	48,073	55,940	61,038	62,834	64,719	61,842	54,438	56,103	1.13
East North Central	46,075	58,869	58,390	61,850	66,034	68,347	59,592	46,616	58,222	1.17
Illinois	43,581	53,468	58,303	63,682	65,232	68,826	63,212	48,953	58,157	1.17
Indiana	44,276	69,636	55,221	54,160	62,938	61,324	52,319	39,737	54,951	1.10
Michigan	52,069	65,266	67,575	76,979	78,650	80,225	67,408	46,240	66,802	1.34
Ohio	48,162	58,290	56,687	59,511	65,015	65,485	56,501	48,761	57,302	1.15
Wisconsin	41,938	52,461	53,542	51,508	54,924	62,436	54,515	45,547	52,109	1.05
West North Central	43,120	48,910	51,400	53,423	54,724	54,168	48,740	37,431	48,990	.98
Iowa	51,125	51,059	59,413	67,661	59,973	59,513	52,561	39,781	55,137	1.11
Kansas	43,142	48,313	46,821	49,615	60,258	52,604	43,382	32,076	47,026	.94
Minnesota	47,494	57,145	64,952	61,773	63,647	64,408	59,915	47,093	58,303	1.17
Missouri	29,144	37,470	39,918	43,616	43,735	44,590	44,095	38,008	40,072	.81
Nebraska	45,568	57,040	46,024	47,577	48,969	51,373	43,900	30,665	46,390	.93
North Dakota	49,188	46,572	55,758	49,863	54,101	54,498	45,228	32,519	48,466	.97
South Dakota	50,082	49,045	49,243	49,822	51,566	52,329	49,008	32,453	47,944	.96

South Atlantic	19,250	25,933	28,495	32,379	34,480	34,417	30,274	24,734	28,745	.58
Delaware	40,541	55,244	55,911	60,413	57,920	65,731	67,737	64,246	58,468	1.17
Florida	25,736	32,021	31,221	40,161	52,097	36,444	33,748	27,635	34,883	.70
Georgia	12,818	15,618	17,436	21,073	21,489	22,335	21,138	18,455	18,801	.38
Maryland	32,437	43,985	47,553	48,719	52,903	55,595	53,846	46,935	47,747	.96
North Carolina	15,620	22,140	26,027	29,334	29,833	30,431	24,153	16,829	24,296	.49
South Carolina	11,916	16,537	21,956	24,934	26,869	28,514	20,823	18,754	21,288	.43
Virginia	20,927	27,869	27,900	28,151	29,641	30,649	28,403	24,835	27,297	.55
West Virginia	29,491	41,370	42,014	51,258	49,558	52,306	45,448	33,904	43,169	.87
East South Central	14,271	18,614	21,129	24,797	27,289	28,657	25,929	20,103	22,600	.45
Alabama	15,361	17,331	19,995	22,673	24,407	26,502	21,994	18,367	20,829	.42
Kentucky	15,270	21,348	25,193	29,436	30,446	32,474	28,763	23,047	25,747	.52
Mississippi	12,365	16,169	16,104	20,162	26,368	25,632	25,802	15,197	19,725	.40
Tennessee	13,733	19,342	22,746	27,093	28,053	30,058	27,355	23,260	23,955	.48
West South Central	23,593	28,136	27,939	30,467	29,991	33,549	31,384	24,775	28,792	.58
Arkansas	13,108	15,014	17,545	21,672	22,616	23,439	19,528	14,470	18,430	.37
Louisiana	26,171	32,025	32,691	34,968	35,872	34,529	31,847	24,423	31,566	.63
Oklahoma	33,214	35,901	38,710	35,823	34,795	42,060	35,091	25,982	35,197	.71
Texas	22,558	28,206	25,440	29,751	28,579	32,446	33,850	27,110	28,493	.57
Mountain	48,741	55,121	55,548	56,500	59,301	59,029	52,449	40,671	53,420	1.07
Arizona	64,253	61,405	67,484	63,324	62,400	64,453	58,442	40,901	60,333	1.21
Colorado	41,672	54,577	58,643	62,579	65,646	65,090	58,985	44,288	56,435	1.13
Idaho	47,038	51,960	51,091	49,137	51,146	52,024	45,462	34,186	47,756	.96
Montana	65,302	66,256	59,309	62,072	63,273	63,558	55,616	43,437	59,853	1.20
Nevada	63,778	75,800	79,524	81,864	75,038	77,500	76,607	65,310	74,428	1.50
New Mexico	34,670	42,606	38,602	40,079	45,039	44,603	41,214	33,864	40,085	.81
Utah	41,655	45,484	45,078	44,039	46,885	47,953	40,296	35,756	43,395	.87
Wyoming	56,327	63,968	70,600	72,301	81,691	72,845	63,706	47,733	66,146	1.33
Pacific	50,251	62,160	62,425	69,766	75,392	77,306	70,779	57,728	65,726	1.32
California	51,758	66,450	66,616	77,314	84,841	85,532	81,488	68,009	72,751	1.46
Oregon	34,675	48,719	48,740	51,693	54,644	59,215	43,213	32,653	46,694	.94
Washington	57,788	59,935	58,878	59,174	60,647	62,248	56,346	40,901	56,990	1.15
United States	37,605	46,584	49,149	52,614	56,127	58,185	53,807	44,101	49,772	1.00

TABLE 19. RELATIVE ABILITY AND EFFORT OF THE STATES TO FINANCE EDUCATION AS RELATED TO ADEQUACY OF FINANCIAL SUPPORT

States	Ability[1]	Effort[2]	Adequacy[3]	Per Cent Decline in Adequacy 1930 to 1934 [4]
1	2	3	4	5
New York	1.85	.86	1.59	10.0
Rhode Island	1.52	.80	1.23	11.8
Nevada	1.44	1.16	1.50	15.7
Massachusetts	1.42	.97	1.39	15.7
Connecticut	1.40	.92	1.28	23.0
California	1.36	1.09	1.46	20.5
New Hampshire	1.36	.89	1.22	15.7
New Jersey	1.34	1.22	1.59	20.5
Delaware	1.30	.88	1.17	2.3
Illinois	1.27	.94	1.17	28.9
Iowa	1.19	.93	1.11	33.2
Maryland	1.17	.82	.96	15.6
Pennsylvania	1.16	.98	1.13	15.9
Michigan	1.10	1.27	1.34	42.4
Ohio	1.10	1.05	1.15	25.5
Wyoming	1.05	1.34	1.33	34.5
Wisconsin	1.01	1.03	1.05	27.1
Washington	1.00	1.15	1.15	34.3
Minnesota	.99	1.21	1.17	26.9
Vermont	.98	1.00	.98	29.2
Nebraska	.98	.96	.93	40.3
South Dakota	.96	1.00	.96	38.0
Maine	.96	.91	.87	24.8
Montana	.95	1.24	1.20	31.7
Oregon	.94	1.04	.94	44.9
Indiana	.90	1.25	1.10	35.2
Missouri	.90	.90	.81	14.8
Kansas	.88	1.09	.94	39.0
Arizona	.81	1.55	1.21	36.5
Colorado	.80	1.47	1.13	32.0
West Virginia	.79	1.21	.87	35.2
Oklahoma	.75	1.04	.71	38.2
Florida	.75	.97	.70	24.2
North Idaho	.74	1.31	.97	40.3
Idaho	.74	1.29	.96	34.3
Louisiana	.65	.99	.63	29.3
Texas	.65	.89	.57	16.4
Virginia	.63	.87	.55	19.0
Utah	.58	1.52	.87	25.5
New Mexico	.55	1.47	.81	24.1
Kentucky	.54	.99	.52	29.0
Tennessee	.53	.93	.48	22.6
North Carolina	.51	1.03	.49	44.7
Georgia	.45	.85	.38	17.6
Arkansas	.45	.84	.37	38.4

TABLE 19 (*Continued*)

States	Ability[1]	Effort[2]	Adequacy[3]	Per Cent Decline in Adequacy 1930 to 1934 [4]
I	2	3	4	5
South Carolina	.44	1.02	.43	34.2
Alabama	.42	1.01	.42	30.7
Mississippi	.33	1.26	.40	40.7
United States	1.00	1.00	1.00	

[1] Ability in column 2 is the average of the indices of relative ability given in columns 2 and 3 of Table 17.
[2] Effort in column 3 is the average of the indices of relative effort given in columns 4 and 5 of Table 17.
[3] Adequacy in column 4 is the index of relative adequacy given in column 11 of Table 18.
[4] The figures given in column 5 indicate the percentage decline in expenditures for current expenses per 1000 units of educational need from 1930 to 1934, according to figures given in columns 7 and 9 of Table 18.

states are arranged in order of ability. The ability of the nation to finance education is given the value 1.00, at the foot of the column. The relative ability of each state is expressed by the figure after its name. The same method is used in columns 3 and 4 to set forth the relative effort made by each state to finance schools, and the relative adequacy of the financial support provided.

The data of Table 19 clearly show that a state's ability to finance education, rather than its effort, determines the adequacy of the support provided. All the states which rank high in ability to finance schools provide a level of financial support distinctly above the average for the country as a whole. This is true regardless of whether these favored states make greater or less than average effort. New York, with 1.85 times the ability to finance schools of the United States as a whole, makes only 86 per cent as much effort to finance schools as the country as a whole, but provides 59 per cent more effective financial support per child to be educated than the average for the country. Mississippi, at the other extreme, with 33 per cent of average ability to finance schools, makes 26 per cent more effort than average, and is able to raise only 40 per cent as much per child as the average for the country. All but five of the twenty-four states most able to finance education provide more than average financial support per unit of educational need, even though half of them make less than average effort to finance education. Only three of the twenty-four states least able to finance education provide more than average financial support, even though fifteen of them are making greater than average effort. Practically all states which rank low in ability to finance schools provide a level of financial support distinctly below the average for the nation. This is true regardless of whether these least able states make greater or less than average effort.

The significance of the foregoing statements is increased by the fact that the data of Table 19 involve the use of the improved methods of measuring taxable capacity and financial resources of the states, described in Chapter III (page 27) as well as the improved technique for measuring educational need (page 28). This technique measures the amount of education to be provided in each state in units of uniform financial significance.

The last column of Table 19 presents data showing the effect of the depression on the schools. The poorer states generally found it necessary to make the largest cuts in financial support between 1930 and 1934. Only five of the twelve richest states reduced their school expenditures per child more than 20 per cent. Nine of the twelve poorest states reduced school expenditures more than 20 per cent between 1930 and 1934.

On the basis of data presented in this and earlier chapters, certain important conclusions concerning the financing of education in the United States are fully justified. The wide differences in the level of financial support provided education in different states are almost wholly the outcome of wide differences in ability to finance education. The disparities in financial support are not primarily due to the failure of some states to make proper effort to finance schools. In fact, states now providing the least adequate financial support for education, as a group, are making greater effort than those providing the most adequate financial support.

The gross inequalities in financial provision for the support of education in different states grow out of fundamental differences in the economic resources and taxpaying capacity of these states. Any attempt to achieve greater equalization of financial support for education in the United States must take account of this fundamental fact.

The primary purpose of this study has been to present facts bearing upon the relation of the ability and the effort of the states to finance education to the adequacy of the financial support which is provided. This purpose has been fulfilled. It is proper, however, to point out some of the broader social implications of the facts as they appear to the authors of the study.

Gross inequalities in educational opportunity now characterize the public schools of the United States. In some areas schools are generously supported and children have rich educational opportunities. In other areas schools are inadequately financed and children are offered the most meager educational opportunities. This fact is abundantly supported by data which appear regularly in statistical surveys of education made by the United States Office of Education. Those who have had opportunity to come in contact with schools in many different sections of the nation need no statistics to support the fact that equality of educational opportunity is an ideal rather than an accomplishment in this country.

Furthermore, it is known that the disparities in educational opportunity are associated with certain cultural lags, of which illiteracy and near-illiteracy are merely the most obvious.[1]

In a dictatorship, where those in possession of power do the thinking for the people, such a situation might not be of great concern. In a democracy, in which the people are supposed to make, or at least to pass on, fundamental decisions of public policy, such a situation cannot be accepted with equanimity. Growing inability to meet the increasingly complex and arduous responsibilities of citizenship must follow upon a situation which denies millions of children adequate educational opportunity.

Under existing policies for the financial support of education in the United States, there is no prospect that educational inequality can be eliminated. This inequality grows out of long-standing and fundamental differences in the economic resources and taxpaying capacity of the states. Any attempt to provide educational opportunity for all children which does not take account of this fundamental fact is foredoomed to failure.

Educational opportunity cannot be provided for all American children by exhorting the states and areas which do not now provide adequate educational facilities to make greater financial effort to support their schools. These states are already making greater effort to pay for the education of their children than does the country as a whole. In spite of the meagerness of their resources, they devote a larger proportion of their income to the financing of schools than do the economically favored states.

Educational opportunity cannot be guaranteed all American children by urging the states that do not now provide adequate schools to

[1] John K. Norton, *The Ability of the States to Support Education*, Chap. IV, pp. 39–60. National Education Association, Washington, D. C., 1926.

put their governmental houses in order. Even the most modern systems of taxation and the most perfect governmental organizations do not create wealth and income. They merely provide a means whereby a portion of wealth and income may be secured and used to finance public enterprises. The tax systems now in effect in the states with meager taxpaying capacity are already securing a larger proportion of total income for the financing of education than is being secured in the economically favored states. Some states have such slender resources that if they allocated to schools all the revenue which could be raised by a modern system of taxes levied at substantial rates, they still could not provide satisfactory educational opportunities for all children.

It is desirable that every state should make the maximum reasonable effort to finance its schools. It is also desirable that every state should raise its public revenue through state tax systems which are well-diversified and equitable. Every state should provide for the spending of the revenue thus raised under a scheme of governmental organization which promises the utmost in economy and efficiency. But even if these desirable ends were achieved tomorrow, millions of children would still be denied reasonable educational opportunity. All the cultural and social liabilities which grow out of such a situation would still exist.

All American children can be guaranteed adequate educational opportunity only if fundamental rather than superficial action is taken. This action must be based on a clear recognition of certain fundamental facts. It must be recognized that the economic productivity of the nation as a whole is large enough to permit every child to attend a good school. It must also be recognized that the economic productivity of some states is not large enough to permit every child to attend a good school. The evidence set forth in this study establishes these facts. Accordingly, action in the direction of providing educational opportunity to all children must involve some pooling of the nation's economic resources.

Appendix

APPENDIX

TABLE A gives the percentage of the economic resources of the nation in each state as indicated by the weighted index of economic resources. Figures are given for each even-numbered year, 1920 to 1934 inclusive. Tables 10 and 11 give the data for 1930 upon which the percentages of weighted economic resources of Table A for 1930 were based, as well as the sources of these data. The per cent of total weighted economic resources given for each year in Table A was calculated by the same method used in arriving at those for 1930.

The percentage of total units of educational need given for each year in Table A is based upon the figures of Table B. In arriving at the number of units of educational need in each state, Ashby, author of the publication cited at the foot of Table B, followed the Mort technique for calculating educational need. The procedure involved the following steps for each state: (1) Average daily attendance in public schools was used as the basic figure. (2) Each high school pupil in average daily attendance was weighted 1.7 times each elementary school pupil—thus taking account of the fact that high school pupils cost 70 per cent more than elementary school pupils on the average. Not only was a state credited with the number of high school pupils in attendance, but each high school pupil was given 70 per cent greater weight than each elementary school pupil because of the cost differential. (3) Total number of average daily attendance units, based on elementary pupil attendance and weighted high school pupil attendance, was then multiplied by Mort's composite index, which corrects for the cost differentials due to degree of sparsity of population and price level or cost of living in each state.

The figures as to relative ability to finance education, given in Table A for each state, were calculated as follows. Using the 1.21 for Connecticut in 1920 as an illustration, this state has 1.47 per cent of the economic resources of the nation (column 2) and 1.21 per cent of the educational need or load of the nation (column 3). Therefore, according to the formula for estimating ability to finance education (resources divided by amount of need, described in Chapter II), 1.47 was divided by 1.21 to give 1.21, the ability figure given for Con-

TABLE A. RELATIVE ABILITY OF THE STATES TO FINANCE EDUCATION, 1920–1934

Based on Weighted Economic Resources per Unit of Educational Need

State and Geographic Division	1920 Per Cent of Total — Weighted Economic Resources	1920 Per Cent of Total — Units of Educational Need	1920 Relative Ability	1922 Per Cent of Total — Weighted Economic Resources	1922 Per Cent of Total — Units of Educational Need	1922 Relative Ability	1924 Per Cent of Total — Weighted Economic Resources	1924 Per Cent of Total — Units of Educational Need	1924 Relative Ability	1926 Per Cent of Total — Weighted Economic Resources	1926 Per Cent of Total — Units of Educational Need	1926 Relative Ability
1	2	3	4	5	6	7	8	9	10	11	12	13
New England	7.77	6.04	1.29	8.03	5.90	1.36	7.64	5.86	1.30	7.36	6.02	1.22
Connecticut	1.47	1.21	1.21	1.52	1.20	1.27	1.53	1.17	1.31	1.54	1.24	1.24
Maine	.63	.71	.89	.66	.69	.96	.61	.68	.90	.60	.65	.92
Massachusetts ..	4.26	3.06	1.39	4.38	2.97	1.47	4.12	2.98	1.38	3.95	3.12	1.27
New Hampshire .	.40	.32	1.25	.42	.30	1.40	.40	.30	1.33	.34	.30	1.13
Rhode Island ...	.69	.42	1.64	.72	.42	1.71	.67	.42	1.60	.63	.43	1.47
Vermont	.32	.32	1.00	.33	.32	1.03	.31	.31	1.00	.30	.28	1.07
Middle Atlantic ...	26.41	18.14	1.46	27.30	17.81	1.53	27.01	17.94	1.51	27.05	18.16	1.49
New Jersey	2.83	2.65	1.07	3.01	2.52	1.19	3.04	2.59	1.17	3.10	2.66	1.17
New York	15.98	8.32	1.92	16.61	8.08	2.06	16.31	8.22	1.98	16.55	8.32	1.99
Pennsylvania ...	7.60	7.17	1.06	7.68	7.21	1.07	7.66	7.13	1.07	7.40	7.18	1.03
East North Central	21.25	19.09	1.11	21.25	18.84	1.13	21.70	19.65	1.10	21.73	19.78	1.10
Illinois	6.90	5.82	1.19	7.04	5.63	1.25	7.19	5.66	1.27	7.07	5.51	1.28
Indiana	2.60	2.84	.92	2.56	2.72	.94	2.59	2.91	.89	2.58	3.04	.85
Michigan	3.55	3.18	1.12	3.63	3.00	1.21	3.87	3.35	1.16	4.04	3.42	1.18
Ohio	5.57	4.91	1.13	5.46	5.14	1.06	5.57	5.23	1.07	5.47	5.28	1.04
Wisconsin	2.63	2.34	1.12	2.56	2.35	1.09	2.48	2.50	.99	2.57	2.53	1.02
West North Central	13.88	14.43	.96	13.36	14.42	.93	13.13	13.77	.95	12.87	13.49	.95
Iowa	3.45	2.67	1.29	3.21	2.74	1.17	3.15	2.56	1.23	3.10	2.46	1.26
Kansas	2.16	2.28	.95	1.95	2.21	.88	1.93	2.26	.85	1.99	2.15	.93
Minnesota	2.27	2.62	.87	2.30	2.58	.89	2.23	2.40	.93	2.22	2.37	.94
Missouri	2.69	3.44	.78	2.62	3.26	.80	2.58	3.14	.82	2.54	3.15	.81
Nebraska	1.69	1.70	.99	1.62	1.72	.94	1.65	1.64	1.01	1.62	1.63	.99
North Dakota ...	.67	.96	.70	.75	1.07	.70	.77	.92	.84	.65	.88	.74
South Dakota ...	.95	.75	1.27	.91	.84	1.08	.82	.85	.96	.75	.85	.88

South Atlantic	8.12	13.19	.62	7.58	12.84	.59	7.68	12.72	.60	7.87	12.81	.61
Delaware	.19	.16	1.19	.18	.16	1.13	.19	.16	1.19	.21	.16	1.31
Florida	.53	.95	.56	.58	.90	.64	.77	.95	.81	1.02	1.16	.88
Georgia	1.39	2.79	.50	1.16	2.78	.42	1.13	2.72	.42	1.10	2.46	.45
Maryland	1.12	1.04	1.08	1.17	1.03	1.14	1.12	1.03	1.09	1.14	1.04	1.10
North Carolina	1.52	2.72	.56	1.49	2.72	.55	1.50	2.72	.55	1.61	2.85	.56
South Carolina	.97	1.94	.50	.79	1.73	.46	.78	1.56	.50	.72	1.63	.44
Virginia	1.25	2.11	.59	1.19	2.05	.58	1.20	2.09	.57	1.18	2.08	.57
West Virginia	1.15	1.48	.78	1.02	1.47	.69	.99	1.49	.66	.89	1.43	.62
East South Central	4.03	8.48	.48	3.86	8.82	.44	3.74	8.27	.45	3.76	7.93	.47
Alabama	.89	2.19	.41	.90	2.25	.40	.90	2.09	.43	.95	1.98	.48
Kentucky	1.24	2.03	.61	1.17	2.22	.53	1.10	2.06	.53	1.05	1.82	.58
Mississippi	.75	1.55	.48	.69	2.00	.35	.66	1.91	.35	.68	1.98	.34
Tennessee	1.15	2.71	.42	1.10	2.35	.47	1.08	2.21	.49	1.08	2.15	.50
West South Central	8.51	10.94	.78	8.06	11.63	.69	8.14	11.45	.71	8.25	11.30	.73
Arkansas	.77	1.95	.39	.82	1.92	.43	.86	1.79	.48	.84	1.66	.51
Louisiana	1.20	1.49	.81	1.03	1.49	.69	.96	1.47	.65	.96	1.41	.68
Oklahoma	2.39	2.29	1.04	2.38	2.44	.98	2.29	2.41	.95	2.42	2.34	1.03
Texas	4.15	5.21	.80	3.83	5.78	.66	4.03	5.78	.70	4.03	5.89	.68
Mountain	2.96	3.99	.74	2.86	3.84	.74	2.80	3.86	.73	2.79	3.86	.72
Arizona	.21	.33	.64	.20	.32	.63	.22	.33	.67	.22	.35	.63
Colorado	.85	1.07	.79	.82	1.08	.76	.76	1.11	.68	.76	1.07	.71
Idaho	.45	.57	.79	.41	.56	.73	.39	.52	.75	.39	.53	.74
Montana	.56	.65	.86	.56	.62	.90	.52	.58	.90	.55	.58	.95
Nevada	.07	.08	.88	.07	.08	.88	.08	.08	1.00	.08	.08	1.00
New Mexico	.18	.43	.42	.17	.36	.47	.17	.39	.44	.18	.39	.46
Utah	.30	.62	.48	.28	.59	.47	.28	.60	.47	.29	.61	.48
Wyoming	.34	.24	1.42	.35	.23	1.52	.38	.25	1.52	.32	.25	1.28
Pacific	7.07	5.71	1.24	7.70	5.90	1.31	8.16	6.48	1.26	8.32	6.65	1.25
California	4.98	3.31	1.50	5.69	3.59	1.58	6.20	4.17	1.49	6.29	4.27	1.47
Oregon	.79	1.00	.79	.78	.92	.85	.77	.92	.84	.83	.95	.87
Washington	1.30	1.40	.93	1.23	1.39	.88	1.19	1.39	.86	1.20	1.43	.84
United States	100.00	100.00	1.00	100.00	100.00	100.00	100.00	100.00	1.00	100.00	100.00	1.00

NOTE: See the discussion in the Appendix accompanying this table for sources of data and methods of calculation for figures given.

TABLE A (Continued). RELATIVE ABILITY OF THE STATES TO FINANCE EDUCATION, 1920-1934

Based on Weighted Economic Resources per Unit of Educational Need

State and Geographic Division	1928			1930			1932			1934			Average 1920-1934 Relative Ability
	Per Cent of Total			Per Cent of Total			Per Cent of Total			Per Cent of Total			
	Weighted Economic Resources	Units of Educational Need	Relative Ability	Weighted Economic Resources	Units of Educational Need	Relative Ability	Weighted Economic Resources	Units of Educational Need	Relative Ability	Weighted Economic Resources	Units of Educational Need	Relative Ability	
1	14	15	16	17	18	19	20	21	22	23	24	25	26
New England	7.39	5.87	1.26	7.56	5.91	1.28	8.10	5.88	1.38	8.06	5.87	1.37	1.31
Connecticut	1.58	1.19	1.33	1.65	1.23	1.34	1.76	1.23	1.43	1.79	1.23	1.46	1.32
Maine	.55	.64	.86	.61	.64	.95	.66	.64	1.03	.63	.64	.98	.94
Massachusetts	3.96	3.02	1.31	3.94	3.02	1.30	4.20	3.01	1.40	4.18	3.01	1.39	1.36
New Hampshire	.37	.30	1.23	.39	.30	1.30	.44	.30	1.47	.44	.29	1.52	1.34
Rhode Island	.63	.44	1.43	.65	.44	1.48	.71	.44	1.61	.72	.44	1.64	1.57
Vermont	.30	.28	1.07	.32	.28	1.14	.33	.26	1.27	.30	.26	1.15	1.09
Middle Atlantic	27.44	18.27	1.50	27.70	18.60	1.49	28.97	18.75	1.55	29.28	18.79	1.56	1.51
New Jersey	3.13	2.74	1.14	3.30	2.78	1.19	3.56	2.80	1.27	3.36	2.82	1.19	1.17
New York	17.04	8.43	2.02	17.06	8.67	1.97	17.94	8.72	2.06	18.60	8.74	2.13	2.02
Pennsylvania	7.27	7.10	1.02	7.34	7.15	1.03	7.48	7.23	1.03	7.32	7.23	1.01	1.04
East North Central	21.33	19.88	1.07	21.28	19.92	1.07	19.93	19.90	1.00	19.26	19.94	.97	1.07
Illinois	6.94	5.71	1.22	6.95	5.68	1.22	6.35	5.54	1.15	6.07	5.53	1.10	1.21
Indiana	2.46	2.96	.83	2.51	2.83	.89	2.40	2.93	.82	2.39	2.92	.82	.87
Michigan	3.98	3.63	1.10	3.89	3.85	1.01	3.68	3.80	.97	3.47	3.85	.90	1.08
Ohio	5.43	5.17	1.05	5.38	5.29	1.02	5.11	5.21	.98	5.03	5.23	.96	1.04
Wisconsin	2.52	2.41	1.05	2.55	2.27	1.12	2.39	2.42	.99	2.30	2.41	.95	1.04
West North Central	12.41	13.07	.95	12.46	12.73	.98	11.83	12.60	.94	11.29	12.51	.90	.95
Iowa	2.89	2.45	1.18	2.92	2.38	1.23	2.68	2.33	1.15	2.42	2.31	1.05	1.20
Kansas	1.94	2.08	.93	1.90	2.05	.93	1.80	2.05	.88	1.74	2.04	.85	.90
Minnesota	2.12	2.33	.91	2.17	2.28	.95	2.13	2.27	.94	2.09	2.26	.92	.92
Missouri	2.45	3.00	.82	2.46	2.88	.85	2.48	2.85	.87	2.43	2.82	.86	.83
Nebraska	1.59	1.58	1.01	1.65	1.48	1.11	1.52	1.54	.99	1.52	1.53	.99	1.00
North Dakota	.67	.82	.82	.59	.86	.69	.57	.80	.71	.53	.80	.66	.73
South Dakota	.75	.81	.93	.77	.80	.96	.65	.76	.86	.56	.75	.75	.96

	1	2	3	4	5	6	7	8	9	10	11	12	13
South Atlantic	7.68	13.02	.59	7.66	12.94	.59	7.97	13.17	.61	8.47	13.16	.64	.61
Delaware	.23	.17	1.35	.22	.17	1.29	.27	.17	1.59	.27	.17	1.59	1.33
Florida	.77	1.24	.62	.76	1.16	.66	.80	1.21	.66	.81	1.23	.66	.69
Georgia	1.09	2.48	.44	1.09	2.42	.45	1.05	2.44	.43	1.25	2.40	.50	.45
Maryland	1.14	1.06	1.08	1.24	1.08	1.15	1.40	1.09	1.28	1.30	1.09	1.19	1.14
North Carolina	1.66	2.93	.57	1.61	2.99	.54	1.63	3.08	.53	1.88	3.10	.61	.56
South Carolina	.71	1.60	.44	.68	1.53	.44	.70	1.56	.45	.81	1.55	.52	.47
Virginia	1.17	2.04	.57	1.19	2.06	.58	1.27	2.08	.61	1.29	2.07	.62	.59
West Virginia	.91	1.50	.61	.87	1.53	.57	.85	1.54	.55	.86	1.55	.55	.63
East South Central	3.85	8.29	.46	3.68	8.13	.45	3.56	8.06	.44	3.79	8.00	.47	.46
Alabama	.96	2.13	.45	.92	2.10	.44	.85	2.14	.40	.92	2.13	.43	.43
Kentucky	1.09	1.99	.55	1.06	1.94	.55	1.07	1.97	.54	1.10	1.96	.56	.56
Mississippi	.72	1.97	.37	.62	1.93	.32	.56	1.81	.31	.61	1.79	.34	.36
Tennessee	1.08	2.20	.49	1.08	2.16	.50	1.08	2.14	.50	1.16	2.12	.55	.49
West South Central	8.64	11.09	.78	8.00	11.07	.72	8.09	10.69	.76	8.20	10.65	.77	.74
Arkansas	.77	1.61	.48	.60	1.48	.41	.59	1.45	.41	.63	1.43	.43	.44
Louisiana	.96	1.47	.65	.93	1.54	.60	.96	1.55	.62	.93	1.54	.60	.66
Oklahoma	2.57	2.33	1.10	2.16	2.32	.93	1.87	2.32	.81	1.82	2.31	.79	.95
Texas	4.34	5.68	.76	4.31	5.73	.75	4.67	5.37	.87	4.82	5.37	.90	.77
Mountain	2.88	3.79	.76	2.85	3.90	.73	2.67	3.92	.68	2.72	3.91	.70	.73
Arizona	.27	.38	.71	.26	.41	.63	.23	.42	.55	.23	.42	.55	.63
Colorado	.74	1.06	.70	.80	1.03	.78	.74	1.02	.73	.71	1.02	.70	.73
Idaho	.41	.52	.79	.41	.52	.79	.38	.51	.75	.39	.51	.76	.76
Montana	.58	.57	1.02	.50	.57	.88	.47	.57	.82	.49	.56	.87	.90
Nevada	.08	.09	.89	.08	.08	1.00	.07	.09	.78	.07	.09	.78	.90
New Mexico	.20	.34	.59	.22	.42	.52	.24	.44	.55	.27	.44	.61	.51
Utah	.30	.60	.50	.30	.60	.50	.29	.61	.48	.28	.61	.46	.48
Wyoming	.30	.23	1.30	.28	.27	1.04	.25	.26	.96	.28	.26	1.08	1.27
Pacific	8.38	6.72	1.25	8.81	6.80	1.30	8.88	7.04	1.26	8.93	7.17	1.25	1.27
California	6.39	4.33	1.48	6.75	4.51	1.50	6.86	4.59	1.49	6.90	4.70	1.47	1.50
Oregon	.76	.94	.81	.79	.86	.92	.77	1.04	.74	.77	1.05	.73	.82
Washington	1.23	1.45	.85	1.27	1.43	.89	1.25	1.41	.89	1.26	1.42	.89	.88
United States	100.00	100.00	1.00	100.00	100.00	1.00	100.00	100.00	1.00	100.00	100.00	1.00	1.00

necticut. This may be interpreted as meaning that Connecticut, for each unit of educational need (child in school, weighted for the cost factors already described), has 21 per cent more economic resources than has the nation as a whole.

The validity of the weighted index of economic resources as a measure of the "economic resources" of a state used in the denominator of the ability formula rests upon these considerations. It takes account of ten important items indicative of economic activity for which reasonably reliable comparable data are available. What these items are and the sources of data concerning them are cited in Table 10.

No claim is made that this weighted index is the best one which might have been developed. Other items and other weightings might have been used. Further research will determine improvements that should be made. Those interested in this problem should consult the studies of Newcomer and Mort cited in Chapter III, both of which present discussion pertinent to the whole question. The purpose of developing this index of economic resources was to make a reasonably satisfactory start. Further research, profiting from the experience gained in calculating the index presented here, will doubtless improve upon the outcome achieved.

The question might be raised as to the validity of the index of economic resources presented in this study. Does it measure what it purports to measure? The answer must be that it does, if the economic items are sufficient in number and of sufficient economic significance to constitute important indications of economic activity, and if they are properly combined. The authors believe that the index presented meets these requirements and that, therefore, it is a valid means of comparing the economic and financial resources of the states. It is the latter which must be measured in the numerator of the ability formula.

One might contend that it would be desirable to compare, or even to validate, the index of economic resources against some measure of the financial resources of the states such as Newcomer's index of taxpaying ability based on six selected taxes, or Chism's estimate of the yield of a modern system of taxes. It is agreed that it is desirable to compare this and other indexes of economic resources with indexes of taxpaying capacity. Such comparison has been made in this study. It is one of the means whereby one may gain a better grasp of the meaning of both types of indexes. The authors do not agree, however, that a carefully developed index of economic resources need be validated against any particular measure of taxpaying capacity. It would be as logical to contend that an index of taxpaying capacity has no value until it is validated against an index of economic resources. Taxpaying capacity does not create economic resources. Rather taxpaying capacity results from economic activity. Furthermore, who would claim that a perfect measure of taxpaying capacity has yet been devised? Chism's estimates employ certain taxes in what he calls a model tax system. Some would not grant that it is a model tax system. They might contend that it gives altogether too much weight to the tax based on tangible property. They might question some of his methods of calculation. Newcomer's index of taxpaying ability employs six selected taxes. Were the right taxes selected? Is the relatively little weight given to the real estate tax defensible? Were the very serious obstacles in the way of arriving at accurate estimates of the value of real estate in each state successfully surmounted?

In the light of the foregoing discussion, the position of the authors of this publication is that economic power or resources, or financial ability or capacity, or whatever one chooses to call the numerator of the ability formula, is far too complex to permit any one method of measuring it to stand alone as sufficient and valid in itself. Experts in the field of mental measurement do not expect to measure intellectual ability through any one single or simple test. Rather, they recognize the complexity of their task and approach it from a variety of angles. Even then, they are none too certain of what their measurements mean.

The economic organization of the United States today is tremendously complex. It is not easy to arrive at a satisfactory means of measuring the economic resources of a state. No one method of doing so will be wholly satisfactory at this period of research. Accordingly, it is desirable to have several, rather than one, means of measuring economic resources or taxpaying capacity or whatever one chooses to call the numerator of the formula used in calculating ability to finance education. By using a variety of approaches to the measurement of this concept we will not only measure it more adequately, but will arrive at a clearer understanding of what the concept is and of how it conditions the ability of a state to pay for the education of its children.

Certain questions might be raised concerning the denominator of the formula used as a basis of calculating ability in Table A. The work which Mort has done has sought to clarify the concept of educational need. At first glance it might be argued that a child is a child; therefore, why complicate the situation? The difficulty is that a child is not a child in terms of the cost of educating him. A child in Nevada fifty miles from any other child costs much more to educate than a child in Connecticut close to thousands of other children. Hence one does not know what the financial cost of educating children is until he knows where the children are. If they live in a section where half the cost of their schooling goes for transportation, then one must spend more per child to purchase a given type of education than if they live in a section where no transportation expenditures are required. Also, if price levels are high, the living costs of the teacher will be high and one must spend more for teachers' salaries than if living costs are low. Only when such factors are taken into account, as by the Mort technique, is it possible to arrive at a method of measuring the size of the educational task of each state in a manner which has financial meaning.

One might criticize the method of calculating educational need in Table B by contending that the total number of children, rather than the number of children actually in public school, should be used as a basis for measuring the educational need of a state. This involves the whole question of how to deal with the fact that a few states have a considerable portion of their children in school, but not in schools supported from public taxation. There is no reason why one cannot take the total number of children as the basis of calculating educational need and then correct for the factors which Mort brings into his technique. It should be noted, however, that Ashby's study points out that if this is done, it will not materially change the relative ability of the states to finance education, nor invalidate the conclusions of a study such as this.[1] Data are presented in this study as to average daily attendance and number of children aged 5–17 years. This will permit one to compare the effect of using the Mort technique for measuring educational need with that gained by using other methods of measuring the size of the educational task of the states. Ashby's study also raises certain other questions concerning the validity of the formulas used in calculating ability and effort which are of interest to the research worker. It does not appear, however, that the solution of any of these questions will result in invalidating the formulas used in this publication.

[1] Lyle Walter Ashby, *The Efforts of the States to Support Education*, pp. 56–57.

TABLE B. NUMBER OF UNITS OF EDUCATIONAL NEED IN EACH STATE,
1920–1934* (in 1000's)

State	1919–20	1921–22	1923–24	1925–26	1927–28	1929–30	1931–32	1933–34
1	2	3	4	5	6	7	8	9
Alabama	499	596	580	575	641	658	712	716
Arizona	75	84	91	102	115	128	138	141
Arkansas	446	507	495	482	484	466	483	483
California	756	949	1,155	1,237	1,304	1,414	1,528	1,583
Colorado	244	286	308	309	319	324	341	344
Connecticut	276	318	323	360	359	385	409	416
Delaware	37	41	45	46	50	52	57	57
Florida	216	238	263	336	373	365	404	414
Georgia	637	735	754	714	748	758	812	809
Idaho	131	149	143	153	157	164	171	172
Illinois	1,328	1,488	1,569	1,598	1,720	1,783	1,843	1,863
Indiana	648	718	806	881	891	888	977	985
Iowa	609	723	709	713	738	748	776	778
Kansas	521	584	627	623	625	642	684	686
Kentucky	463	586	571	528	598	610	657	661
Louisiana	340	395	408	408	444	484	516	520
Maine	162	181	187	189	194	200	213	215
Maryland	238	272	284	302	320	338	364	367
Massachusetts ...	699	785	827	903	908	947	1,003	1,015
Michigan	725	793	927	992	1,092	1,207	1,265	1,296
Minnesota	597	681	666	686	703	716	757	761
Mississippi	353	528	528	574	593	606	602	604
Missouri	784	863	871	912	904	903	950	950
Montana	149	164	162	167	172	181	190	190
Nebraska	389	454	455	473	477	466	512	514
Nevada	18	20	21	22	26	26	28	29
New Hampshire ..	72	79	82	87	89	93	98	99
New Jersey	604	665	719	771	824	871	931	950
New Mexico	97	94	108	114	102	131	145	147
New York	1,899	2,135	2,278	2,412	2,539	2,720	2,904	2,945
North Carolina ..	621	720	753	826	884	937	1,026	1,044
North Dakota	218	283	256	255	247	271	267	268
Ohio	1,120	1,360	1,449	1,531	1,557	1,659	1,734	1,761
Oklahoma	523	645	669	677	703	728	771	777
Oregon	228	242	254	274	284	270	347	352
Pennsylvania	1,636	1,907	1,976	2,081	2,139	2,243	2,409	2,435
Rhode Island	95	111	117	124	131	137	147	149
South Carolina ...	442	458	432	472	481	481	519	521
South Dakota	170	223	235	247	244	252	252	254
Tennessee	619	622	613	624	663	677	712	716
Texas	1,189	1,527	1,601	1,706	1,712	1,797	1,787	1,809
Utah	142	157	166	178	182	188	203	205
Vermont	74	85	86	81	84	87	88	88
Virginia	479	543	580	604	613	646	694	696
Washington	320	368	385	414	436	448	471	477
West Virginia	338	389	414	414	452	481	513	521
Wisconsin	533	621	692	733	725	711	807	813
Wyoming	55	62	70	73	68	84	85	86
United States	22,814	26,434	27,710	28,983	30,114	31,371	33,302	33,682

* Data for 1920–32 are from Lyle W. Ashby, *The Efforts of the States to Support Education*, p. 20. National Education Association, Washington, D. C., 1936. Data for 1933–34 were estimated. Units of educational need were calculated by the application of Mort's index of educational need.

TABLE C. RELATIVE ABILITY OF THE STATES TO FINANCE EDUCATION,
1930

Based on Yield from Six Taxes and Number of Children Aged 5–17

State and Geographic Division	Estimated Tax Yield[1] (In 1,000,000's)	Number of Children Aged 5-17 [2]	Tax Yield per Child Aged 5-17 [3]	Relative Ability[4] (U. S. = 1.00)
1	2	3	4	5
New England	$ 378.0	1,964,958	$192.4	1.25
Connecticut	88.3	402,773	219.2	1.43
Maine	24.6	195,796	125.6	.82
Massachusetts	209.4	999,696	209.5	1.37
New Hampshire	14.7	109,241	134.6	.88
Rhode Island	30.9	169,889	181.9	1.19
Vermont	10.1	87,563	115.3	.75
Middle Atlantic	1,605.0	6,327,984	253.6	1.65
New Jersey	233.8	985,274	237.3	1.55
New York	990.0	2,792,806	354.5	2.31
Pennsylvania	381.2	2,549,904	149.5	.97
East North Central	1,020.1	6,092,323	167.4	1.09
Illinois	354.0	1,770,315	200.0	1.30
Indiana	101.3	783,553	129.3	.84
Michigan	196.2	1,195,057	164.2	1.07
Ohio	263.7	1,599,554	164.9	1.07
Wisconsin	104.9	743,844	141.0	.92
West North Central	490.1	3,365,523	145.6	.95
Iowa	104.4	614,740	169.8	1.11
Kansas	68.4	476,464	143.6	.94
Minnesota	92.0	675,090	140.0	.91
Missouri	126.0	860,094	146.5	.96
Nebraska	55.6	357,648	155.5	1.01
North Dakota	19.4	204,010	95.1	.62
South Dakota	24.3	195,477	124.3	.81
South Atlantic	400.5	4,592,386	87.2	.57
Delaware	92.7	57,610	1,609.1	10.49
Florida	41.7	378,446	110.2	.72
Georgia	35.0	894,723	39.1	.25
Maryland	58.7	402,562	145.8	.95
North Carolina	52.0	1,030,317	50.5	.33
South Carolina	18.0	592,047	30.4	.20
Virginia	51.9	716,445	72.4	.47
West Virginia	50.5	520,236	97.1	.63
East South Central	141.5	2,935,749	48.2	.31
Alabama	29.0	817,365	35.5	.23
Kentucky	41.2	753,063	54.7	.36
Mississippi	20.0	613,148	32.6	.21
Tennessee	51.3	752,173	68.2	.44
West South Central	249.3	3,489,536	71.4	.47
Arkansas	24.2	560,048	43.2	.28
Louisiana	30.4	606,318	50.1	.33
Oklahoma	57.5	695,334	82.7	.54
Texas	137.2	1,627,836	84.3	.55

TABLE C (*Continued*)

State and Geographic Division	Estimated Tax Yield[1] (In 1,000,000's)	Number of Children Aged 5–17 [2]	Tax Yield per Child Aged 5–17 [3]	Relative Ability[4] (U. S. = 1.00)
1	2	3	4	5
Mountain	143.1	1,004,328	142.5	.93
Arizona	16.0	117,218	136.5	.89
Colorado	37.9	260,748	145.4	.95
Idaho	15.8	127,201	124.2	.81
Montana	22.7	141,349	160.6	1.05
Nevada	12.8	19,007	673.4	4.39
New Mexico	9.1	127,324	71.5	.47
Utah	17.4	153,686	113.2	.74
Wyoming	11.4	57,795	197.2	1.29
Pacific	401.5	1,710,431	234.7	1.53
California	299.2	1,139,224	262.6	1.71
Oregon	39.1	214,179	182.6	1.19
Washington	63.2	357,028	177.0	1.15
United States	4,829.1	31,483,218	153.4	1.00

[1] The estimated tax yield from these six taxes: Personal income, real estate, business income, corporation organization, stock transfer, and severance (which were selected by Newcomer for the index of ability) is from Mabel Newcomer, *An Index of the Taxpaying Ability of State and Local Governments*, p. 54, Table VI, col. 2. Bureau of Publications, Teachers College, Columbia University, 1935.

[2] The data of column 2 as to number of children aged 5–17 in 1930 are from the *Biennial Survey of Education, 1928–1930*, Vol. II, p. 44, Table 4, col. 3. United States Office of Education, Bulletin, 1931, No. 20. Government Printing Office, Washington, D. C., 1932.

[3] Figures in column 4 are obtained by dividing figures in column 2 by those in column 3.

[4] Relative ability of the several states to finance education is related to the ability of the United States, which is assigned the value 1.00. The figures in column 5 are obtained by dividing each of the figures in column 4 by 153.4.

Table C compares the relative ability of the states to support education, based on the Newcomer index of taxpaying ability for 1930, arrived at by estimating the yield of the following six taxes: personal income, real estate, business income, corporation organization, stock transfer, and severance. The general position of most of the states with reference to ability to support schools is similar in this table to that occupied in tables dealing with the ability of the states to finance education in Chapters II and III. There are some exceptions. Delaware seems to possess substantially higher ability to support schools in Table C than in Tables 5, 7, and 12. This is due mainly to differences in the nature of the items used by Newcomer in measuring financial ability.[2] The greater financial ability of Delaware is due mainly to the inclusion of the corporation organization tax in the Newcomer index. Since Delaware would receive 42 per cent of the estimated national yield of this tax, the effect of its inclusion is to increase greatly the apparent economic ability of this state. Because of

[2] Mabel Newcomer, *An Index of the Taxpaying Ability of State and Local Governments*, pp. 39–41.

TABLE D. EXPENDITURES OF THE STATES FOR CURRENT EXPENSES OF
PUBLIC EDUCATION LESS REVENUE RECEIVED FROM
FEDERAL AID AND SUBSIDIES, 1934

State and Geographic Division	Current Expenses[1]	Federal Aid for		Subsidies from Educational Foundations	Current Expenses Less Columns 3, 4 and 5
		Rural Teachers	Vocational Education		
1	2	3	4	5	6
New England	$ 116,555,202	$ ..	$ 378,604	$ ..	$ 116,176,598
Connecticut ...	23,444,098	..	77,078	..	23,367,020
Maine	7,803,011	..	51,263	..	7,751,748
Massachusetts ..	66,905,157	..	189,023	..	66,716,134
New Hampshire	5,489,053	..	18,046	..	5,471,007
Rhode Island ..	9,415,674	..	31,505	..	9,384,169
Vermont	3,498,209	..	11,689	..	3,486,520
Middle Atlantic ..	454,879,396	..	1,215,372	..	453,664,024
New Jersey	71,789,161	..	172,855	..	71,616,306
New York	250,032,878	..	542,592	..	249,490,286
Pennsylvania ...	133,057,357	..	499,925	..	132,557,432
East North Central	314,894,825	317,234	1,411,384	..	313,166,207
Illinois	91,818,435	225,800	392,521	..	91,200,114
Indiana	39,329,061	..	187,950	..	39,141,111
Michigan	60,276,738	91,434	258,282	..	59,927,022
Ohio	86,292,654	..	424,958	..	85,867,696
Wisconsin	37,177,937	..	147,673	..	37,030,264
West North Central	159,692,621	1,207,814	863,970	..	157,620,837
Iowa	31,071,253	8,354	112,837	..	30,950,062
Kansas	22,125,448	..	121,029	..	22,004,419
Minnesota	36,059,327	57,596	163,281	..	35,838,450
Missouri	36,861,955	535,400	218,284	..	36,108,271
Nebraska	15,943,443	80,057	101,862	..	15,761,524
North Dakota ..	9,138,349	334,362	89,218	..	8,714,769
South Dakota ..	8,492,846	192,045	57,459	..	8,243,342
South Atlantic ...	115,038,912	4,273,591	1,022,840	196,875	109,545,606
Delaware	3,688,808	..	27,257	..	3,661,551
Florida	12,211,844	620,794	138,837	11,451	11,440,762
Georgia	16,703,459	1,599,057	159,570	14,546	14,930,286
Maryland ..?..	17,312,285	..	82,189	5,150	17,224,946
North Carolina .	18,296,364	500,000	199,712	28,012	17,568,640
South Carolina .	10,280,279	341,603	124,104	44,001	9,770,571
Virginia	18,261,378	702,566	180,098	93,715	17,284,999
West Virginia ..	18,284,495	509,571	111,073	..	17,663,851
East South Central	58,400,547	4,469,733	634,056	78,279	54,218,479
Alabama	15,281,193	1,971,982	116,300	41,724	13,151,187
Kentucky	15,748,876	337,552	177,055	..	15,234,269
Mississippi	10,665,915	1,320,555	130,155	36,555	9,178,650
Tennessee	17,704,563	839,644	210,546	..	16,654,373
West South Central	93,202,247	3,448,209	743,862	90,994	88,919,182
Arkansas	7,844,132	696,078	117,531	41,138	6,989,385

TABLE D (*Continued*)

State and Geographic Division	Current Expenses[1]	Federal Aid for		Subsidies from Educational Foundations	Current Expenses Less Columns 3, 4 and 5
		Rural Teachers	Vocational Education		
1	2	3	4	5	6
Louisiana	13,787,671	956,073	114,876	17,116	12,699,606
Oklahoma	21,499,759	1,176,888	126,707	8,390	20,187,774
Texas	50,070,685	619,170	384,748	24,350	49,042,417
Mountain	54,467,929	686,257	334,813	6,000	53,440,859
Arizona	5,909,717	76,121	66,720	..	5,766,876
Colorado	15,378,576	58,981	84,197	..	15,235,398
Idaho	5,931,755	15,404	36,645	..	5,879,706
Montana	8,385,843	91,289	41,637	..	8,252,917
Nevada	1,926,408	15,864	16,983	..	1,893,561
New Mexico ...	5,289,343	272,218	33,302	6,000	4,977,823
Utah	7,464,375	104,184	30,421	..	7,329,770
Wyoming	4,181,912	52,196	24,908	..	4,104,808
Pacific	139,202,015	133,172	407,027	..	138,661,816
California	107,917,132	..	259,633	..	107,657,499
Oregon	11,661,899	105,387	62,292	..	11,494,220
Washington	19,622,984	27,785	85,102	..	19,510,097
United States	1,507,333,694	14,536,010	7,011,928	372,148	1,485,413,608

[1] Current expenses include the items of general control, instruction, operation of plant, maintenance, auxiliary agencies (such as libraries, promotion of health, transportation of pupils, compulsory attendance, etc.) and fixed charges (such as pensions, rent, insurance, etc.). Expenditures of state departments of education as well as those of local schools are included in this total. Data are from *Statistics of State School Systems, 1933–34*, Bulletin, 1935, No. 2, pp. 82–83. U. S. Office of Education, 1936.

the favorable incorporation laws which Delaware has enacted, the state is in a position at the present time to realize substantial revenue from such a tax, and does realize such revenue. On the other hand, the business activities carried on by nation-wide corporations, which avail themselves of Delaware's incorporation statutes, are mainly carried on outside the state. Other states, by offering certain inducements, might be successful in attracting more big corporations to incorporate within their borders, with increased revenue for granting the privilege, and would enlarge their taxpaying ability accordingly. Revenue from this source would not affect the total taxpaying ability of large states, however, as much as it does a small state such as Delaware. No dogmatic decision can be made as to the desirability of using the corporation organization tax in measuring taxpaying ability. Arguments both for and against its inclusion may be offered, according to the point of view held. Eventually, it is probable that the Federal Government will take over the incorporation of large concerns doing interstate business. This was recommended as long ago as

WEALTH, CHILDREN, EDUCATION

TABLE E. EXPENDITURES OF THE STATES FOR CURRENT
RAISED BY THE STATES

(In thousands

State and Geographic Division	1920		1922		1924		1926	
	Amount	%	Amount	%	Amount	%	Amount	%
1	2	3	4	5	6	7	8	9
New England	$ 68,756	8.02	$ 92,069	7.48	$ 102,363	7.51	$ 110,762	7.26
Connecticut	13,617	1.59	18,069	1.47	20,450	1.50	23,435	1.54
Maine	5,852	.68	7,673	.62	8,232	.60	8,766	.57
Massachusetts ..	37,878	4.42	51,666	4.20	57,868	4.24	61,179	4.01
New Hampshire.	3,567	.42	4,512	.37	5,111	.38	5,603	.37
Rhode Island ..	4,376	.51	6,092	.49	6,773	.50	7,545	.49
Vermont	3,466	.40	4,057	.33	3,929	.29	4,234	.28
Middle Atlantic ..	192,403	22.43	288,909	23.46	337,178	24.73	376,155	24.67
New Jersey	32,762	3.82	45,969	3.73	54,705	4.01	63,189	4.14
New York	94,296	10.99	151,265	12.28	171,935	12.61	185,946	12.20
Pennsylvania ...	65,345	7.62	91,675	7.45	110,538	8.11	127,020	8.33
East North Central	200,611	23.38	293,167	23.81	317,818	23.30	354,709	23.26
Illinois	57,876	6.75	79,560	6.46	91,478	6.71	101,764	6.67
Indiana	28,691	3.34	49,999	4.06	44,508	3.26	47,715	3.13
Michigan	37,750	4.40	51,756	4.20	62,642	4.59	76,363	5.01
Ohio	53,941	6.29	79,274	6.44	82,139	6.02	91,112	5.97
Wisconsin	22,353	2.60	32,578	2.65	37,051	2.72	37,755	2.48
West North Central	141,778	16.52	186,397	15.14	196,295	14.40	208,831	13.70
Iowa	31,135	3.63	36,916	3.00	42,124	3.09	48,242	3.16
Kansas	22,477	2.62	28,215	2.29	29,357	2.15	30,910	2.03
Minnesota	28,354	3.30	38,916	3.16	43,258	3.17	42,376	2.78
Missouri	22,849	2.66	32,337	2.63	34,769	2.55	39,778	2.61
Nebraska	17,726	2.07	25,896	2.10	20,941	1.54	22,504	1.48
North Dakota ..	10,723	1.25	13,180	1.07	14,274	1.05	12,715	.83
South Dakota ..	8,514	.99	10,937	.89	11,572	.85	12,306	.81
South Atlantic ...	57,903	6.75	88,070	7.15	101,298	7.43	120,255	7.88
Delaware	1,500	.18	2,265	.18	2,516	.18	2,779	.18
Florida	5,559	.65	7,621	.62	8,211	.60	13,494	.88
Georgia	8,165	.95	11,479	.93	13,147	.96	15,046	.99
Maryland	7,720	.90	11,964	.97	13,505	.99	14,713	.96
North Carolina .	9,700	1.13	15,941	1.29	19,598	1.44	24,230	1.59
South Carolina .	5,267	.61	7,574	.62	9,485	.70	11,769	.77
Virginia	10,024	1.17	15,133	1.23	16,182	1.19	17,003	1.12
West Virginia ..	9,968	1.16	16,093	1.31	18,654	1.37	21,221	1.39
East South Central	27,601	3.21	43,407	3.52	48,428	3.55	57,058	3.74
Alabama	7,665	.89	10,329	.84	11,597	.85	13,037	.85
Kentucky	7,070	.82	12,510	1.01	14,385	1.06	15,542	1.02
Mississippi	4,365	.51	8,537	.69	8,503	.62	11,573	.76
Tennessee	8,501	.99	12,031	.98	13,943	1.02	16,906	1.11
West South Central	58,936	6.87	86,489	7.02	88,650	6.51	99,720	6.54
Arkansas	5,846	.68	7,612	.62	8,685	.64	10,446	.68
Louisiana	8,898	1.04	12,650	1.02	13,338	.98	14,267	.94
Oklahoma	17,371	2.02	23,156	1.88	25,897	1.90	24,252	1.59
Texas	26,821	3.13	43,071	3.50	40,730	2.99	50,755	3.33

EXPENSES OF PUBLIC EDUCATION LESS FUNDS NOT
THEMSELVES, 1920–1934

of dollars)

| 1928 | | 1930 | | 1932 | | 1934 | | Average 1920–1934 |
| Amount | % | Amount | % | Amount | % | Amount | % | % |
10	11	12	13	14	15	16	17	18
$ 124,662	7.38	$ 132,234	7.24	$ 133,700	7.46	$ 116,177	7.82	7.53
25,782	1.53	28,079	1.54	29,646	1.65	23,367	1.57	1.55
9,514	.56	9,586	.52	9,783	.54	7,752	.52	.58
70,438	4.17	73,815	4.04	73,084	4.08	66,716	4.49	4.21
5,819	.34	6,098	.33	6,394	.36	5,471	.37	.37
8,723	.52	9,788	.54	10,389	.58	9,384	.63	.53
4,386	.26	4,868	.27	4,404	.25	3,487	.24	.29
431,041	25.50	483,930	26.51	508,578	28.38	453,663	30.54	25.78
73,229	4.33	82,628	4.53	87,277	4.87	71,616	4.82	4.28
223,411	13.22	256,138	14.03	272,324	15.20	249,490	16,80	13.42
134,401	7.95	145,164	7.95	148,977	8.31	132,557	8.92	8.08
395,211	23.38	427,035	23.38	394,854	22.04	313,166	21.08	22.96
112,199	6.64	122,717	6.72	116,500	6.50	91,200	6.14	6.57
56,078	3.32	54,456	2.98	51,116	2.85	39,141	2.64	3.20
85,886	5.08	96,831	5.30	85,271	4.76	59,927	4.03	4.68
101,228	5.99	108,639	5.95	97,973	5.47	85,868	5.78	5.99
39,820	2.35	44,392	2.43	43,994	2.46	37,030	2.49	2.52
215,504	12.75	216,565	11.86	204,609	11.42	157,620	10.61	13.30
44,260	2.62	44,516	2.44	40,787	2.28	30,950	2.08	2.79
37,661	2.23	33,772	1.85	29,673	1.66	22,004	1.48	2.04
44,744	2.65	46,116	2.53	45,356	2.53	35,838	2.41	2.82
39,536	2.34	40,265	2.20	41,890	2.34	36,108	2.43	2.47
23,358	1.38	23,940	1.31	22,477	1.25	15,762	1.06	1.52
13,363	.79	14,769	.81	12,076	.67	8,715	.59	.88
12,582	.74	13,187	.72	12,350	.69	8,243	.56	.78
135,177	8.00	139,666	7.65	132,873	7.42	109,547	7.38	7.44
2,896	.17	3,418	.19	3,861	.22	3,662	.25	.19
19,432	1.15	13,302	.73	13,634	.76	11,441	.77	.77
16,074	.95	16,968	.93	17,164	.96	14,930	1.01	.96
16,929	1.00	18,791	1.03	19,600	1.10	17,225	1.16	1.01
26,372	1.56	28,514	1.56	24,780	1.38	17,569	1.18	1.39
12,924	.76	13,715	.75	10,807	.60	9,771	.66	.68
18,170	1.08	19,799	1.08	19,712	1.10	17,285	1.16	1.14
22,400	1.33	25,159	1.38	23,315	1.30	17,664	1.19	1.30
68,087	4.03	73,179	4.00	69,567	3.88	54,218	3.65	3.70
15,645	.92	17,438	.96	15,660	.87	13,151	.88	.88
18,207	1.08	19,809	1.08	18,897	1.05	15,234	1.03	1.02
15,636	.93	15,533	.85	15,533	.87	9,179	.62	.73
18,599	1.10	20,349	1.11	19,477	1.09	16,654	1.12	1.07
100,261	5.93	116,584	6.39	113,410	6.33	88,919	5.99	6.44
10,946	.65	10,946	.60	9,432	.53	6,989	.47	.61
15,927	.94	16,712	.92	16,433	.92	12,700	.86	.95
24,461	1.45	30,620	1.68	27,055	1.51	20,188	1.36	1.67
48,927	2.89	58,306	3.19	60,490	3.37	49,042	3.30	3.21

TABLE E

State and Geographic Division	1920		1922		1924		1926	
	Amount	%	Amount	%	Amount	%	Amount	%
I	2	3	4	5	6	7	8	9
Mountain	44,403	5.18	56,003	4.55	59,381	4.36	63,167	4.14
Arizona	4,819	.56	5,158	.42	6,141	.45	6,459	.42
Colorado	10,168	1.19	15,609	1.27	18,062	1.32	19,337	1.27
Idaho	6,162	.72	7,742	.63	7,306	.54	7,518	.49
Montana	9,730	1.14	10,866	.88	9,608	.71	10,366	.68
Nevada	1,148	.13	1,516	.12	1,670	.12	1,801	.12
New Mexico ...	3,363	.39	4,005	.33	4,169	.31	4,569	.30
Utah	5,915	.69	7,141	.58	7,483	.55	7,839	.51
Wyoming	3,098	.36	3,966	.32	4,942	.36	5,278	.35
Pacific	65,527	7.64	96,907	7.87	111,990	8.21	134,299	8.81
California	39,129	4.56	63,061	5.12	76,942	5.64	95,637	6.27
Oregon	7,906	.92	11,790	.96	12,380	.91	14,164	.93
Washington	18,492	2.16	22,056	1.79	22,668	1.66	24,498	1.61
United States	857,918	100.00	1,231,418	100.00	1,363,401	100.00	1,524,902	100.00

the administration of President Taft. A bill on the subject was introduced twenty-five years ago in the Senate of the United States. A measure looking to the same end is currently being proposed.

The justification of including or excluding such a tax in an index of taxpaying ability depends upon the purpose for which this index is intended. If the desire is an equitable tax system, such a tax cannot be included. This is obvious if one gives thought to current practice. Corporations now pick out a state which makes it "easy" to incorporate, and incorporate there. Delaware is such a state par excellence. In Wilmington, in one office building, 10,000 corporations are listed on the wall directory in the lobby. Corporations doing nation-wide business, such as Radio Corporation of America, National Dairy, and the Pullman Company have their "home offices" in this building. They have no home offices elsewhere in the legal sense. Incorporated in Delaware, a corporation can do business all over the world, even though no directors live in the state and no stockholders' meetings are ever held there. Everything is made very convenient, provided the incorporation fee is paid.

Obviously such an arrangement comes as near to being a racket as an equitable tax situation. So long as such conditions are permitted to continue, they must be taken account of in practical measurements of taxpaying capacity. This is properly done in the Newcomer index.

(*Continued*)

1928		1930		1932		1934		Average 1920–1934
Amount	%	Amount	%	Amount	%	Amount	%	%
10	11	12	13	14	15	16	17	18
67,663	4.00	72,369	3.95	68,236	3.80	53,442	3.60	4.20
7,176	.42	8,250	.45	8,065	.45	5,767	.39	.45
20,941	1.24	21,089	1.15	20,114	1.12	15,235	1.02	1.20
8,030	.48	8,532	.47	7,774	.43	5,880	.40	.52
10,883	.64	11,504	.63	10,567	.59	8,253	.55	.73
1,951	.12	2,015	.11	2,145	.12	1,894	.13	.12
4,594	.27	5,843	.32	5,976	.33	4,978	.34	.32
8,533	.50	9,017	.49	8,180	.46	7,330	.49	.53
5,555	.33	6,119	.33	5,415	.30	4,105	.28	.33
152,594	9.03	164,817	9.02	166,048	9.27	138,662	9.33	8.65
110,633	6.55	120,942	6.62	124,514	6.95	107,658	7.25	6.12
15,519	.92	15,988	.87	14,995	.84	11,494	.77	.89
26,442	1.56	27,887	1.53	26,539	1.48	19,510	1.31	1.64
1,690,230	100.00	1,825,329	100.00	1,791,875	100.00	1,485,414	100.00	100.00

On the other hand, if one wishes to arrive at a measure of ability to pay taxes, which assumes an equitable federal and state system of taxation, one would not include such practical sources of state revenue.

This study is more interested in the long-term measurement of theoretical taxpaying ability, assuming equitability in tax structure, than in immediate practicalities. Hence it gives less extensive consideration to the Newcomer index, which was concerned with immediate practical taxpaying capacity. The same consideration applies to the index of taxpaying ability developed by Mort in his volume on *Federal Support for Public Education*. This valuable practical instrument accepts the Newcomer index as the criterion of taxpaying ability.

A stock transfer tax is also included in the Newcomer index. Such a tax adds materially to the taxpaying ability of New York State and a few other states. New York would realize approximately 85 per cent of the total estimated yield of such a tax. Here again we have a situation in which circumstances permit a few states, New York especially, to realize tax revenue based upon nation-wide economic activity, namely, the purchase and sale of securities in connection with investment and speculation. These states have no peculiar claim to this revenue. Once again the case for or against including such a tax in measuring ability depends upon the purpose in mind.

A severance tax on petroleum and natural gas is included in the

TABLE F. RELATIVE EFFORT OF THE STATES TO FINANCE EDUCATION, 1920-1934

Based on Ratio of Current Expenditures for Education and Weighted Economic Resources

	1920			1922			1924			1926		
	Per Cent of Total		Rela-tive Ef-fort	Per Cent of Total		Rela-tive Ef-fort	Per Cent of Total		Rela-tive Ef-fort	Per Cent of Total		Rela-tive Ef-fort
State and Geographic Division	Amount Spent for Educa-tion	Weighted Eco-nomic Resources		Amount Spent for Educa-tion	Weighted Eco-nomic Resources		Amount Spent for Educa-tion	Weighted Eco-nomic Resources		Amount Spent for Educa-tion	Weighted Eco-nomic Resources	
1	2	3	4	5	6	7	8	9	10	11	12	13
New England	8.02	7.77	1.03	7.48	8.03	.93	7.51	7.64	.98	7.26	7.36	.99
Connecticut	1.59	1.47	1.09	1.47	1.52	.97	1.50	1.53	.98	1.54	1.54	1.00
Maine	.68	.63	1.08	.62	.66	.94	.60	.61	.98	.57	.60	.95
Massachusetts	4.42	4.26	1.04	4.20	4.38	.96	4.24	4.12	1.03	4.01	3.95	1.02
New Hampshire	.42	.40	1.05	.37	.42	.88	.38	.40	.95	.37	.34	1.09
Rhode Island	.51	.69	.74	.49	.72	.68	.50	.67	.75	.49	.63	.78
Vermont	.40	.32	1.25	.33	.33	1.00	.29	.31	.94	.28	.30	.93
Middle Atlantic	22.43	26.41	.85	23.46	27.30	.86	24.73	27.01	.92	24.67	27.05	.91
New Jersey	3.82	2.83	1.35	3.73	3.01	1.24	4.01	3.04	1.32	4.14	3.10	1.34
New York	10.99	15.98	.69	12.28	16.61	.74	12.61	16.31	.77	12.20	16.55	.74
Pennsylvania	7.62	7.60	1.00	7.45	7.68	.97	8.11	7.66	1.06	8.33	7.40	1.13
East North Central	23.38	21.25	1.10	23.81	21.25	1.12	23.30	21.70	1.07	23.26	21.73	1.07
Illinois	6.75	6.90	.98	6.46	7.04	.92	6.71	7.19	.93	6.67	7.07	.94
Indiana	3.34	2.60	1.28	4.06	2.56	1.59	3.26	2.59	1.26	3.13	2.58	1.21
Michigan	4.40	3.55	1.24	4.20	3.63	1.16	4.59	3.87	1.19	5.01	4.04	1.24
Ohio	6.29	5.57	1.13	6.44	5.46	1.18	6.02	5.57	1.08	5.97	5.47	1.09
Wisconsin	2.60	2.63	.99	2.65	2.56	1.04	2.72	2.48	1.10	2.48	2.57	.97
West North Central	16.52	13.88	1.19	15.14	13.36	1.13	14.40	13.13	1.10	13.70	12.87	1.06
Iowa	3.63	3.45	1.05	3.00	3.21	.93	3.09	3.15	.98	3.16	3.10	1.02
Kansas	2.62	2.16	1.21	2.29	1.95	1.17	2.15	1.93	1.11	2.03	1.99	1.02
Minnesota	3.30	2.27	1.45	3.16	2.30	1.37	3.17	2.23	1.42	2.78	2.22	1.25
Missouri	2.66	2.69	.99	2.63	2.62	1.00	2.55	2.58	.99	2.61	2.54	1.03
Nebraska	2.07	1.69	1.22	2.10	1.62	1.30	1.54	1.65	.93	1.48	1.62	.91
North Dakota	1.25	.67	1.87	1.07	.75	1.43	1.05	.77	1.36	.83	.65	1.28
South Dakota	.99	.95	1.04	.89	.91	.98	.85	.82	1.04	.81	.75	1.08

South Atlantic	6.75	8.12	.83	7.15	7.58	.94	7.43	7.68	.97	7.88	7.87	1.00
Delaware	.18	.19	.95	.18	.18	1.00	.18	.19	.95	.18	.21	.86
Florida	.65	.53	1.23	.62	.58	1.07	.60	.77	.78	.88	1.02	.86
Georgia	.95	1.39	.68	.93	1.16	.80	.96	1.13	.85	.99	1.10	.90
Maryland	.90	1.12	.80	.97	1.17	.83	.99	1.12	.88	.96	1.14	.84
North Carolina	1.13	1.52	.74	1.29	1.49	.87	1.44	1.50	.96	1.59	1.61	.99
South Carolina	.61	.97	.63	.62	.79	.78	.70	.78	.90	.77	.72	1.07
Virginia	1.17	1.25	.94	1.23	1.19	1.03	1.19	1.20	.99	1.12	1.18	.95
West Virginia	1.16	1.15	1.01	1.31	1.02	1.28	1.37	.99	1.38	1.39	.89	.56
East South Central	3.21	4.03	.80	3.52	3.86	.91	3.55	3.74	.95	3.74	3.76	.99
Alabama	.89	.89	1.00	.84	.90	.93	.85	.90	.94	.85	.95	.89
Kentucky	.82	1.24	.66	1.01	1.17	.86	1.06	1.10	.96	1.02	1.05	.97
Mississippi	.51	.75	.68	.69	.69	1.00	.62	.66	.94	.76	.68	1.12
Tennessee	.99	1.15	.86	.98	1.10	.89	1.02	1.08	.94	1.11	1.08	1.03
West South Central	6.87	8.51	.81	7.02	8.06	.87	6.51	8.14	.80	6.54	8.25	.79
Arkansas	.68	.77	.88	.62	.82	.76	.64	.86	.74	.68	.84	.81
Louisiana	1.04	1.20	.87	1.02	1.03	.99	.98	.96	1.02	.94	.96	.98
Oklahoma	2.02	2.39	.85	1.88	2.38	.79	1.90	2.29	.83	1.59	2.42	.66
Texas	3.13	4.15	.75	3.50	3.83	.91	2.99	4.03	.74	3.33	4.03	.83
Mountain	5.18	2.96	1.75	4.55	2.86	1.59	4.36	2.80	1.56	4.14	2.79	1.48
Arizona	.56	.21	2.67	.42	.20	2.10	.45	.22	2.05	.42	.22	1.91
Colorado	1.19	.85	1.40	1.27	.82	1.55	1.32	.76	1.74	1.27	.76	1.67
Idaho	.72	.45	1.60	.63	.41	1.54	.54	.39	1.38	.49	.39	1.26
Montana	1.14	.56	2.04	.88	.56	1.57	.71	.52	1.37	.68	.55	1.24
Nevada	.13	.07	1.86	.12	.07	1.71	.12	.08	1.50	.12	.08	1.50
New Mexico	.39	.18	2.17	.33	.17	1.94	.31	.17	1.82	.30	.18	1.67
Utah	.69	.30	2.30	.58	.28	2.07	.55	.28	1.96	.51	.29	1.76
Wyoming	.36	.34	1.06	.32	.35	.91	.36	.38	.95	.35	.32	1.09
Pacific	7.64	7.07	1.08	7.87	7.70	1.02	8.21	8.16	1.01	8.81	8.32	1.06
California	4.56	4.98	.92	5.12	5.69	.90	5.64	6.20	.91	6.27	6.29	1.00
Oregon	.92	.79	1.16	.96	.78	1.23	.91	.77	1.18	.93	.83	1.12
Washington	2.16	1.30	1.66	1.79	1.23	1.46	1.66	1.19	1.39	1.61	1.20	1.34
United States	100.00	100.00	1.00	100.00	100.00	1.00	100.00	100.00	1.00	100.00	100.00	1.00

TABLE F (Continued). RELATIVE EFFORT OF THE STATES TO FINANCE EDUCATION, 1920–1934

Based on Ratio of Current Expenditures for Education and Weighted Economic Resources

State and Geographic Division	1928 Per Cent of Total			1930 Per Cent of Total			1932 Per Cent of Total			1934 Per Cent of Total			Average 1920–1934
	Amount Spent for Education	Weighted Economic Resources	Relative Effort	Amount Spent for Education	Weighted Economic Resources	Relative Effort	Amount Spent for Education	Weighted Economic Resources	Relative Effort	Amount Spent for Education	Weighted Economic Resources	Relative Effort	Relative Effort
1	14	15	16	17	18	19	20	21	22	23	24	25	26
New England	7.38	7.39	1.00	7.24	7.56	.96	7.46	8.10	.92	7.82	8.06	.97	.97
Connecticut	1.53	1.58	.97	1.54	1.65	.93	1.65	1.76	.94	1.57	1.79	.88	.97
Maine	.56	.55	1.02	.52	.61	.85	.54	.66	.82	.52	.63	.83	.93
Massachusetts ...	4.17	3.96	1.05	4.04	3.94	1.03	4.08	4.20	.97	4.49	4.18	1.07	1.02
New Hampshire .	.34	.37	.92	.33	.39	.85	.36	.44	.82	.37	.44	.84	.93
Rhode Island	.52	.63	.83	.54	.65	.83	.58	.71	.82	.63	.72	.88	.79
Vermont	.26	.30	.87	.27	.32	.84	.25	.33	.76	.24	.30	.80	.92
Middle Atlantic	25.50	27.44	.93	26.51	27.70	.96	28.38	28.97	.98	30.54	29.28	1.04	.93
New Jersey	4.33	3.13	1.38	4.53	3.30	1.37	4.87	3.55	1.37	4.82	3.36	1.43	1.35
New York	13.22	17.04	.78	14.03	17.06	.82	15.20	17.94	.85	16.80	18.60	.90	.79
Pennsylvania	7.95	7.27	1.09	7.95	7.34	1.08	8.31	7.48	1.11	8.92	7.32	1.22	1.08
East North Central .	23.38	21.33	1.10	23.38	21.28	1.10	22.04	19.93	1.11	21.08	19.26	1.09	1.10
Illinois	6.64	6.94	.96	6.72	6.95	.97	6.50	6.35	1.02	6.14	6.07	1.01	.97
Indiana	3.32	2.46	1.35	2.98	2.51	1.19	2.85	2.40	1.19	2.64	2.39	1.10	1.27
Michigan	5.08	3.98	1.28	5.30	3.89	1.36	4.76	3.68	1.29	4.03	3.47	1.16	1.24
Ohio	5.99	5.43	1.10	5.95	5.38	1.11	5.47	5.11	1.07	5.78	5.03	1.15	1.11
Wisconsin	2.35	2.52	.93	2.43	2.55	.95	2.46	2.39	1.03	2.49	2.30	1.08	1.01
West North Central.	12.75	12.41	1.03	11.86	12.46	.95	11.42	11.83	.97	10.61	11.29	.94	1.05
Iowa	2.62	2.89	.91	2.44	2.92	.84	2.28	2.68	.85	2.08	2.42	.86	.93
Kansas	2.23	1.94	1.15	1.85	1.90	.97	1.66	1.80	.92	1.48	1.74	.85	1.05
Minnesota	2.65	2.12	1.25	2.53	2.17	1.17	2.53	2.13	1.19	2.41	2.09	1.15	1.28
Missouri	2.34	2.45	.96	2.20	2.46	.89	2.34	2.48	.94	2.43	2.43	1.00	.98
Nebraska	1.38	1.59	.87	1.31	1.65	.79	1.25	1.52	.82	1.06	1.52	.70	.94
North Dakota	.79	.67	1.18	.81	.59	1.37	.67	.57	1.18	.59	.53	1.11	1.35
South Dakota	.74	.75	.99	.72	.77	.94	.69	.65	1.06	.56	.56	1.00	1.02

South Atlantic	8.00	1.04	7.68	7.65	7.66	1.00	7.42	7.97	.93	7.38	8.47	.87	.95
Delaware	.17	.74	.23	.19	.22	.86	.22	.27	.81	.25	.27	.93	.89
Florida	1.15	.49	.77	.73	.76	.96	.76	.80	.95	.77	.81	.95	1.04
Georgia	.95	.87	1.09	.93	1.09	.85	.96	1.05	.91	1.01	1.25	.81	.83
Maryland	1.00	.88	1.14	1.03	1.24	.83	1.10	1.40	.79	1.16	1.30	.89	.84
North Carolina	1.56	.94	1.66	1.56	1.61	.97	1.38	1.63	.85	1.18	1.88	.63	.87
South Carolina	.76	1.07	.71	.75	.68	1.10	.60	.70	.86	.66	.81	.81	.90
Virginia	1.08	.92	1.17	1.08	1.19	.91	1.10	1.27	.87	1.16	1.29	.90	.94
West Virginia	1.33	1.46	.91	1.38	.87	.59	1.30	.85	1.53	1.19	.86	1.38	1.40
East South Central	4.03	1.05	3.85	4.00	3.68	1.09	3.88	3.56	1.09	3.65	3.79	.96	.98
Alabama	.92	.96	.96	.96	.92	1.04	.87	.85	1.02	.88	.92	.96	.97
Kentucky	1.08	.99	1.09	1.08	1.06	1.02	1.05	1.07	.98	1.03	1.10	.94	.92
Mississippi	.93	1.29	.72	.85	.62	1.37	.87	.56	1.55	.62	.61	1.02	1.12
Tennessee	1.10	1.02	1.08	1.11	1.08	1.03	1.09	1.08	1.01	1.12	1.16	.97	.97
West South Central	5.93	.69	8.64	6.39	8.00	.80	6.33	8.09	.78	5.99	8.20	.73	.78
Arkansas	.65	.84	.77	.60	.60	1.00	.53	.59	.90	.47	.63	.75	.84
Louisiana	.94	.98	.96	.92	.93	.99	.92	.96	.90	.86	.93	.92	.96
Oklahoma	1.45	.56	2.57	1.68	2.16	.78	1.51	1.87	.81	1.36	1.82	.75	.75
Texas	2.89	.67	4.34	3.19	4.31	.74	3.37	4.67	.72	3.30	4.82	.68	.76
Mountain	4.00	1.39	2.88	3.95	2.85	1.39	3.80	2.67	1.42	3.60	2.72	1.32	1.49
Arizona	.42	1.56	.27	.45	.26	1.73	.45	.23	1.96	.39	.23	1.70	1.95
Colorado	1.24	1.68	.74	1.15	.80	1.44	1.12	.74	1.51	1.02	.71	1.44	1.55
Idaho	.48	1.17	.41	.47	.41	1.15	.32	.38	1.13	.40	.39	1.03	1.28
Montana	.64	1.10	.58	.63	.50	1.26	.59	.47	1.26	.55	.49	1.12	1.37
Nevada	.12	1.50	.08	.11	.08	1.38	.12	.07	1.71	.13	.07	1.86	1.63
New Mexico	.27	1.35	.20	.32	.22	1.45	.33	.24	1.38	.34	.27	1.26	1.63
Utah	.50	1.67	.30	.49	.30	1.63	.46	.29	1.59	.49	.28	1.75	1.84
Wyoming	.33	1.10	.30	.33	.28	1.18	.30	.25	1.20	.28	.28	1.00	1.06
Pacific	9.03	1.08	8.38	9.02	8.81	1.02	9.27	8.88	1.04	9.33	8.93	1.04	1.04
California	6.55	1.03	6.39	6.62	6.75	.98	6.95	6.86	1.01	7.25	6.90	1.05	.98
Oregon	.92	1.21	.76	.87	.79	1.10	.84	.77	1.09	.77	.77	1.00	1.14
Washington	1.56	1.27	1.23	1.53	1.27	1.20	1.48	1.25	1.18	1.31	1.26	1.04	1.32
United States	100.00	1.00	100.00	100.00	100.00	1.00	100.00	100.00	1.00	100.00	100.00	1.00	1.00

Newcomer index to take account of large incomes resulting from relatively small investments. It is argued that this situation calls for a special tax other than that based on property valuation. The effect of the inclusion of this item in the index is to increase substantially the apparent taxable ability of several states. Oklahoma and Texas have their ability increased 13 per cent and 6 per cent respectively by the inclusion of this tax. A few other states are affected, but to a smaller degree.

Table D presents the method of calculating educational expenditures used in the adequacy formula of Chapter V, and gives sources of data. Table E gives the amounts expended for schools in each state from 1920 to 1924, for even-numbered years, calculated as illustrated in Table D. The percentages which the expenditures for education are of total expenditures are also given in Table D for each year and each state. These percentages in turn are used in Table F, along with the percentage of economic resources found in each state, in calculating relative effort to finance schools. The formula used in calculating effort is discussed in Chapter IV. The figures of Table F may be further explained by the following illustration: Connecticut expends 1.59 per cent of the total expenditures of the nation for education. It has 1.47 per cent of the financial resources of the country. Therefore, according to the effort formula described in Chapter IV (amount expended for education divided by financial resources), Connecticut's effort to finance schools is 9 per cent greater than the average for the country (1.59 divided by 1.47 equals 1.09).

Bibliography

BIBLIOGRAPHY

American Engineering Council, Committee on Elimination of Waste in Industry. *Waste in Industry.* Federated American Engineering Societies, Washington, D. C., 1921. 409 pp.

Ashby, Lyle W. *The Efforts of the States to Support Education.* National Education Association, Washington, D. C., 1936. 63 pp.

Ayres, Leonard P. *An Index Number of State School Systems.* Russell Sage Foundation, New York, 1920. 70 pp.

Chism, Leslie L. *Economic Ability of the States to Finance Public Schools.* Bureau of Publications, Teachers College, Columbia University, New York, 1936. 169 pp.

Columbia University Commission. *Economic Reconstruction.* Columbia University Press, New York, 1934. 250 pp.

Harris, William T. "Some of the Conditions Which Cause Variation in the Rate of School Expenditures in Different Localities." *Proceedings, 1905,* Vol. 44, pp. 195–213. National Education Association, Washington, D. C., 1906.

Leven, Maurice, Moulton, Harold G., and Warburton, Clark. *America's Capacity to Consume.* Brookings Institution, Washington, D. C., 1934. 272 pp.

Loeb, Harold, Director. *Report of the National Survey of Potential Product Capacity.* New York City Housing Authority, New York, 1936. 358 pp.

Mort, Paul R. *Federal Support for Public Education.* Bureau of Publications, Teachers College, Columbia University, New York, 1936. 334 pp.

Mort, Paul R. *State Support for Public Education.* National Survey of School Finance. American Council on Education, Washington, D. C., 1933. 496 pp.

Moulton, Harold G. *Formation of Capital.* Brookings Institution, Washington, D. C., 1935. 207 pp.

Moulton, Harold G. *Income and Economic Progress.* Brookings Institution, Washington, D. C., 1935. 191 pp.

National Advisory Committee on Education. *Federal Relations to Education.* American Council on Education, Washington, D. C., 1931. 2 vols.

National Industrial Conference Board. *Cost of Government in the United States, 1933–35.* The Board, 247 Park Avenue, New York, 1936. 98 pp.

National Tax Association. *Second Report on a Plan of a Model System of State and Local Taxation.* Wickersham Printing Company, Lancaster, Pa., 1933. 68 pp.

Newcomer, Mabel. *An Index of Taxpaying Ability of State and Local Governments.* Bureau of Publications, Teachers College, Columbia University, New York, 1935. 85 pp.

Norton, John K. *The Ability of the States to Support Education.* National Education Association, Washington, D. C., 1926. 88 pp.

Norton, John K. "American Educational Finance." Chapter VI in *Taxation and Public Policy* (edited by Paul Studenski). Richard R. Smith, New York, 1936.

Nourse, Edwin G. and Associates. *America's Capacity to Produce.* Brookings Institution, Washington, D. C., 1934. 608 pp.

Report of the National Conference on the Financing of Education. Conference held under the auspices of the Joint Commission on the Emergency in Education. Department of Superintendence, Washington, D. C., 1933. 78 pp.

Strayer, George D. and Haig, Robert M. *The Financing of Education in the State of New York.* Educational Finance Inquiry Commission, Vol. 1. The Macmillan Company, New York, 1923. 205 pp.

U. S. Department of Commerce, Bureau of Foreign and Domestic Commerce. *National Income in the United States, 1929–35.* Government Printing Office, Washington, D. C., 1936. 304 pp.

DATE DUE

	JAN 9 1994		